Paper Wings Over Japan

Kites

Kites

Edited by Scott Skinner and Ali Fujino

With contributions by
Tal Streeter
Scott Skinner
Masaaki Modegi
Tsutomu Hiroi

Paper Wings Over Japan

Thames and Hudson

Dedicated to
David and Dorothea Checkley

629.13332 KITES 1997

Kites : paper wings over Japa

First published in paperback in the United States of America in 1997 by Thames and Hudson Inc., 500 Fifth Avenue, New York, New York 10110

First published in Great Britain in 1997 by Thames and Hudson Ltd, London

Library of Congress Catalog Card Number: 96-61423

British Library Cataloguing-in-Publication Data:
A catalogue record for this book is available from the British Library.

ISBN 0-500-27942-X

Published by arrangement with The Drachen Foundation, 1907 Queen Anne Avenue North, Seattle, Washington 98109

Edited by Lorna Price
Designed by Ed Marquand and John Hubbard with assistance by Randalee Maddox
Produced by Marquand Books, Inc.
Printed and bound by C & C Offset Printing Co., Hong Kong

Front cover, clockwise from top left: *tombi* kite by Kazue Tanaka, Skinner Collection; *yakko* kite by Yanase, Streeter Collection; *yakko* kite by Teizo Hashimoto, Checkley Collection, World Kite Museum

Back cover: Edo kite with *nami usagi* motif, by Teizo Hashimoto, collection The Tokyo Kite Museum

Inside covers: Page from one of kitemaker Katsutaka Murooka's sketchbooks

Page 2: *top* Sambaso dancer kite by Masaaki Sato, Skinner Collection; *bottom* Tero wave detail from a Sagara fighter kite, Streeter Collection

Page 3: *Ukiyo-e* woodblock print depicting actor Onoe Kikugoro in the kite dance of Yatsukodo, artist unknown, Skinner Collection

Photo Credits
All photographs by Scott Skinner except as indicated: Ali Fujino, pp. 78, 86 (third from top); Tsutomu Hiroi, pp. 17, 24, 63, 67, 72; Joe Manfredini, p. 85 (third from top); courtesy Masaaki Modegi, p. 76 (top); George Peters, pp. 26, 62, 64–65, 68, 69; Wolfgang Schimmelpfennig, p. 74; Tal Streeter, front cover (top right), pp. 2 (bottom), 15, 21; Gary W. Taylor, front cover (bottom), pp. 41 (top), 44, 48, 50 (top), 52, 71; courtesy The Tokyo Kite Museum, back cover, pp. 42, 46, 47, 53, 57, 59, 70.

Contents

Rectangular kite featuring the religious figure Daruma. Shirone Kite Museum

Acknowledgments

Many skilled and caring hands played a part in making this book.

David Checkley's spirit and example informed the entire project; our travels with Dave and Dorothea Checkley continue to have a lasting impact. For encouragement, cooperation, and participation on many levels, we thank Tal Streeter, Masaaki Modegi, and Tsutomu Hiroi. Their insight and friendship have been critical to this project's success.

The staff of the Tokyo Kite Museum, especially Mr. Modegi and Terauki Tsutsumi, along with Kay Buesing and the staff of the World Kite Museum have assisted by lending kites and photographs and by providing much-needed information. Kazuo Tamura of the Shirone Kite Museum has inspired us all with his unwavering enthusiasm and dedication. The Japan Kite Association and its members have provided untold inspiration by their devotion to preserving old kite traditions and encouraging new ones.

We also wish to thank the artists and craftsmen who appear in this book, whose skilled and caring hands both create and promote Japanese kites. Tokuko Sato, Nobuhiku Yoshizumi, Katsutaka Murooka, Masaaki Sato, Satoshi Hashimoto, Toranosuke Watanabe, Takeshi Nishibayashi, and all the others mentioned or pictured were our gateways to the world of Japanese kites.

The organization of data and elements for this book could not have been done without the help of Ben Ruhe and Jo Nilsson of the Drachen Foundation and the technical assistance of Matthew Sutton and Gary W. Taylor. Manuscript editing by Lorna Price and design and production by Ed Marquand and the staff of Marquand Books ensured the highest professional standards; their expertise proved invaluable.

By sharing information or expertise the following people have contributed to the success of this project: Dan Kurahashi, Valerie Govig, Pierre Fabre, George Peters, and Linda Johnston Murosako have written and spoken of their Japanese kite experiences and introduced many to specific people, places, and kites. Nina McGuinness, Rainer Rauhut, Ron and Julie Burnham, John Stevenson, and the staff of Honeychurch Antiques have helped to find, document, and preserve the Japanese prints in the Skinner collection.

We thank you one and all for the parts you have played in putting this book together and getting it into the hands of prospective kite lovers around the world.

—Scott Skinner and Ali Fujino

A View from the West

Scott Skinner

I have flown kites for over twenty years, but I was introduced to Japanese kites at an unlikely event. In 1984, while attending my first American Kitefliers Association convention, my eyes were opened to the vast universe of kites. At an evening auction of kite-related objects, overpowered by auction fever, I became a willing buyer of any number of "artifacts" from the convention. I little knew at the time how much one of them would change my life.

Late that evening, a self-published book in a plain brown wrapper was offered for bid: David Kung's *Japanese Kites: A Vanishing Art.* A glimpse inside revealed hand-painted renderings of Japanese kites, and my mind was made up! After what seemed like furious bidding, the book was mine, and I could study my treasure. Later, as I read the text, I became convinced that Japanese kites were dead. Here was a book, written in 1962, that chronicled a number of very old kitemakers who seemed to have in common only one thing: no one in their family would carry on this tradition. Instead of being uplifted by the beauty of this simple book, I was saddened by the words of these artists:

I am afraid that kite making has arrived at a hopeless state, and I am sure that my kites will also disappear very soon.

—Jiroji Fukuda, Tobata, Kyushu

I think that kite-flying, which is performed regardless of the cold, is the healthiest sport for making one's heart broad, pure, and bright. It is essential and very sound play to foster among the younger generation who will be responsible for Japan's future. But these days, it seems that kites are gradually disappearing from sight, while other playthings, which are apt to lead children into bad conduct, sell well.

—Kaiichi Kinoshita, Takamatsu, Shikoku

Before the war, there were about ten houses specializing in kite making here [Sanjo]; now only three remain. . . . My eldest son became a physician. Such being the case, kite making is no longer a profitable business.

—Seijiro Sudo, Masae Sudo, Sanjo, Niigata

Here was evidence that this older generation—many born before the turn of the century—would be the last to make traditional Japanese kites. But hope glimmered in my mind as I read and reread another book. In Tal Streeter's *Art of the Japanese Kite,* stories of Japanese kitemakers of the 1970s convinced me that not all was lost. Kite festivals with lives hundreds of years long were continuing, kites could be seen as fine art instead of simple toys, and a small cadre of enthusiasts was keeping the interest in kites alive.

Seeing the bold images and elegant geometric shapes of the kites illustrated in Streeter's book convinced me that the Western kite world of deltas, diamonds, and box kites had neglected this long tradition. Since I had already decided that American patchwork patterns could be used with great effect on kites, it seemed natural that Japanese kite shapes would be the ideal platform for them. I was inspired by the traditions of the American quilters and the Japanese kitemakers, but I was bound to neither. I could use the bright, vibrant colors of ripstop nylon with frames made of fiberglass or carbon fiber. I could also let people know how wonderful these Japanese kites were. Now, over ten years later, Japanese kite shapes are being produced by kitemakers all over the world. And at home in Japan, a new generation of kitemakers is using new materials as well as old to produce the timeless designs of their region.

Five years after making my first Japanese kite (I foolishly chose an Edo kite), I traveled to Japan to see kites for myself. After years of trying to decipher some of these kites' secrets, one look at a real example revealed a world of information. I learned that the Edo kite's long, graceful bridles are not simply a thing of beauty, but are entirely functional, adding drag to the kite and acting as long shock absorbers when the ferocious beach wind pounds the kite. My admiration turned to amazement as, in almost every kite style, I discovered some refinement that I'd had no idea about: the bridles on the Edo, the simple two-point bridle on a Sagara fighter or a Kerori, the tapered spine of a *rokkaku*, all carefully placed to balance the kite. I also had no idea how lucky I was, when at that year's Japan Kite Association meeting, I saw the entire spectrum of Japanese kites—Edo, *rokkaku*, Shirone, *tombi, semi-* and *abu-dako*. Only later on the same trip did I fully come to understand that kite traditions are regional or local. In Sagara, for instance, only the type of kite specific to that locale is flown during the festival. It's the same in Hamamatsu, Shirone, Nagasaki, and Ikazaki: "kite" in these cities is synonymous with *their* kite.

Seeing local kites in their historical environment gave me a better idea of the skill of their makers and flyers. Fighting kites of Japan should be compared only with others of the same type. In comparing their agility to fighting kites of Korea or India, you might think less of them, but seeing them fly with others of their type is a thrill. Subtle differences in design or flying skill make huge differences in who wins the contest. The *ho-dako* of Ikazaki flies in a herky-jerky, anything-but-graceful way, but when many are flown together, the skills of the individual flyers are fully displayed.

Today at kite festivals all over the world, another Japanese fighting kite—the *rokkaku*—is flown in a new variation of the kite battles of Sanjo, Niigata. Tactics vary from the refined to the heavy-handed, but cutting, ensnaring, or forcing opponents' kites to the ground has captured the imagination of kite flyers everywhere. The contest has come full circle: in international kite festivals in Japan, foreign kite flyers are asked to participate in a *rokkaku* battle of modern kites made of ripstop nylon and carbon-fiber rods. This is the type of evolution present today in the kite world. In Japan there are still kitemakers who use only traditional materials and techniques, but there are also accomplished amateurs who use contemporary nontraditional materials to duplicate and refine traditional designs. Sport kites are bringing young people to Japanese kite festivals and into Japanese kite associations. I am optimistic that many of them will eventually turn to traditional designs. They may well bring with them modern materials instead of following the traditions of past kitemakers, but this is the natural evolution of any craft. The Japanese kites of the twenty-first century may not be similar to those that David Kung fell in love with in the early 1960s, but I have no doubt that their meticulous craftsmanship and artistic traditions will be passed on.

This book is not intended to be the definitive work on Japanese kites. Instead it sets out to present many of the facts, images, and lore that have captured the imagination of kite flyers all over the world. We also hope that it becomes a gateway to the world of kites in Japan: only through seeing Japanese kites in their home environments can you truly appreciate them. Attending a festival in Japan is unlike any other experience. It may be loud, dirty, and chaotic, or peaceful and serene, but it is always unforgettable.

pages 10–11: Miniature kites by Kazuo Inoue from the *Courtesan* series.
Each approx. 15 × 20 cm. Skinner Collection

Rising Kite with a Kabuki Star. Left panel of an *ukiyo-e* woodblock print triptych
by Kunimasa Baido (1773–1810). Skinner Collection

High Art: Keeping Ancient Asian Kitemaking Traditions Alive in Modern Japan

Tal Streeter

The First Kite

A kite needn't be more than a few sticks of wood and a scrap of paper hanging upside down in the sky at the end of a long string; at the other end on the ground holding this long string, a hand. The genius of the first kite lay in the discovery of the absolute necessity of simplicity and lightness married to principles of aerodynamics, though a scientific explanation of the kite's miraculous powers of flight would not come for thousands of years. The flight of this first kite was undeniably one of the great moments of human history. Over time, kites would stir our imaginations and give us hope that we too might one day fly like the birds. Indeed, we would learn to climb and sail in the sky beneath great wings that were modeled on these early kite creations.

It is often hypothesized that the origin of the kite lies in China. No one can know for sure, but I have come to believe that the first kites very likely came from the region of Malaysia, Indonesia, and the South Pacific. Perhaps they were fabricated from a leaf or leaves woven together, made rigid by pieces of bamboo or a reedlike stick, and attached to a flying line—either a single natural-fiber thread or several threads twined together. Such leaf kites are still seen in this part of the world. We can be certain that leaves preceded the invention of woven silk and then paper, the materials used in the Chinese kites most often credited as "first." The intrinsic fragility and the impermanence of the materials from which the first kite and its flying line were crafted accounts for its disappearance and the elusiveness of its origins.

What can we know for certain about this ancient kite? Only this: The first kite with a long flying line attached sailed out into an ocean sky, a place where no man, woman, or child had ever ventured. At the other end of the kite's umbilical cord, receiving the messages of the great void, was a human hand.

Belying its relatively uncomplicated appearance, the humble kite is the first human-made object capable of sustained, controlled flight. That they are able to fly upside down suggests they are a bit more than meets the eye. In actuality the humblest kite, large or small, is quite a sophisticated flying machine. It seems reasonable to imagine that the ancient kite should now seem irrelevant everywhere throughout the modern world—a piece of antiquated, nearly useless history in a period when anyone able to come up with the price of an airline ticket takes for granted the commonplace of jet travel around the globe. But this is not the case. Inexplicably, almost mysteriously, people everywhere are drawn to the ancient pleasures of their country's kites. In more recent times, when kites have become almost a synonym for childhood, otherwise fully mature, well-adjusted adults willingly

New Year's Day Landscape of Edo. Center panel of an *ukiyo-e* woodblock
print triptych by Chikanobu Utagawa (1836–1912). Skinner Collection

lend their hands, their energy, and increasing amounts of time (and money) to holding innumerable
kite lines climbing up into the sky. Whatever theory explains this fascination, the certain pleasure
of kite flying is readily observable in every kite flyer's face—adults and children alike—what kite enthusiasts have come to recognize as "the kite smile."

We can speculate that this kite smile must be at least partially drawn from the living energy of
sky, sun, and clouds. For kite flyers, a vicarious romp in the sky lifts the weight of earthbound trials
and tribulations. The sky/kite energy entering the kite flyer's fingertips is a very tangible sensation,
though it may be as subtle as the tickle of a light breeze crossing the skin or as strong as the power
of a huge dog lunging on its leash, pulling with such force that kite flyers must dig in their heels to
keep from being dragged across their flying fields. Exciting or tranquilizing, the string-borne messages that come down to us out of the sky are based on a variety of rich kite ingredients.

Were today's kites perceived only as utilitarian objects, we might not find them appearing with
such frequency in books and museums whose mission is to call the public's attention to art. (See
Appendix B: Kite Museums with Japanese Kite Collections.) In Asia not just kite paintings but the
forms of kites are increasingly modified as well, either in the service of newly invented aerodynamic
qualities or in the service of art. This is also true in the West. Unlike the airplane, which has enjoyed

its life as a relatively unsullied, utilitarian, and functional structure free of decoration, the functional kite and its decoration have long accompanied one another in the sky.

In their earliest incarnations Asian kites were employed in the service of religion. Kites traveled in the distant sky, the home of the gods, where requests might be received and favors more readily granted. After religious iconography, came kites bearing images celebrating godlike historical figures. There was also, inevitably it seems, a period early on when kites were employed as instruments of war. Then, perhaps for their longest term of history, they were flown safely in the hands of children, enjoyed as toys. Today, kites are a favored toy of adults (children, of course, are still in the picture), and they are increasingly viewed not just as toys, or a hobby, or sport pastime, but as objects that bring a special pleasure into one's life. From time to time, here and there, artists have found in them an intriguing vehicle, a medium for artistic expression. Kite art and the fine arts, painting and sculpture, have tended to follow the same pathways, from the sacred (religious), to the historical (the royal court, legends, and military heroes), to the profane (anything which entertains or captures the imagination). Of course this oversimplifies the rich tapestry of kites as they first appeared in Asia and then spread throughout the world. Today, a host of countries lay claim to special kites and unique kite-flying traditions.

The Japanese Kite

Many contemporary Western kite enthusiasts first recognized the potential and the excitement of kites through the special qualities of the kites of Japan. There was a bit of serendipity involved in the Japanese kite's rise to preeminence in the West. As we became more culturally sophisticated, we discovered that our appreciation of kites could have emerged through the kite lore and contemporary life of kites in China, Korea, India, Thailand, Malaysia, the islands of Indonesia, and the islands of the South Pacific. All these places had fascinating kites and kite histories, and today have exciting modern-day kites and kite activities. But Japan caught our attention first. And yet today, though we know more about the wider history of Asian kites, few would disagree that the Japanese still number among the world's foremost kite champions. The breadth and quality of their kite forms, imaginative imagery, and exhilarating kite-centered festivals and celebrations add an incomparable zest and joy to the fabric of Japanese life.

The kites that fly above Japan range in scale from those best viewed with a magnifying glass to mammoth kites weighing tons and flown by teams strung out along thick rope flying lines. Some of the world's largest kites are still made in Japan of traditional Asian materials, bamboo and handmade paper. Some of these kites bear legends as old as they are fascinating, and are flown in community-wide kite festivals, many with histories unbroken back to the seventeenth century. In addition to

Raising an *odako* (giant) kite at the Hoshubana kite festival.

their loving attention to maintaining traditions, modern-day Japanese kitemakers are at the cutting edge of contemporary kite innovation. In many respects, this is an unprecedented situation. The old-fashioned kite of bamboo and paper and the high-tech kite of ripstop nylon and carbon-fiber spars lie side by side, figuratively speaking, on the shelves of fancy department stores, along with Japan's latest Sony products.

As recently as twenty-five years ago, with the emergence of Japan as one of the world's preferred suppliers of appealing automobiles and electronic consumer goods, the prognosis for the continuing good health of Japan's kites was less than optimistic. It seemed certain that the three- to four-hundred-year-old traditions maintained by a small number of aging kitemakers would scarcely find customers for this product, let alone young people willing to dedicate their lives to this antique popular art form. Many admirers in the West believed that Japanese kites, as much as they loved them, must surely follow a path into decline. Thus it came as no small surprise that things turned around so dramatically; in Japan, kites hold their own with the newest model Japanese transistor radio and television set. If anything, kites are stronger than ever there; the audience for kites and the number of fine kitemakers seem to grow at an exponential rate.

The reason for this longevity is to be found in the way Japanese kites are created in modern times. Instead of being the exclusive responsibility of an ever-diminishing handful of artists, their continued vigor is now championed by ever-larger groups of kite enthusiasts. They have organized kite clubs in their communities and sponsored festival events and kitemaking workshops in schools and community centers, where the skills and pleasures of kitemaking and flying are passed on to everyone—men, women, and children, from the age of seven to over seventy. If Japan's current enthusiasm for kites is any indication, it seems certain kites can only grow in importance there—with the rest of the world as enthusiastic partners—in the years to come.

Kites in Early Japanese Historical Documents

Kites were first documented entering Japan from China, via Korea, in the first millennium—sometime around the Nara period (A.D. 645–794). Though they conveyed a remnant of science and technology, religion, and general skullduggery (war and other aberrations), for the Japanese, kites were from the beginning a vehicle of wonder and a celebration of joy.

The *Hizen no Kuni fudoki,* a gazeteer of the Nara period, and the *Nihongi* (A.D. 720; *Chronicles of Japan from the Earliest Times to A.D. 697*), both written in Chinese characters, contain the first extant evidence of the existence of kites in the Japanese archipelago. The earliest recording in the Japanese language of a word for kite occurs in the *Wamyo ruiju sho,* a Japanese dictionary compiled in the Shohei era (A.D. 931–938). Though written in a modified version of classical Chinese, it gives the Japanese pronunciation of words. Japanese pronunciation of the Chinese characters in essence formed a new word; the meaning or definition, however, remained constant in both languages. The entry for "kite" has two sets of Chinese characters with Japanese translations, each describing an object made of paper in the shape of a hawk—*shiroshi* (paper, venerable hawk), and *shien* (paper hawk) that "rides the wind and flies well."

Ancient Japanese (and Chinese) paper-hawk kites most likely had small bodies and pocketed wings or, in the shape of a T, longer bodies and either pocketed or flat wings. The T-shaped kite is relatively simple in construction. Its excellent aerodynamic design ensures its ability to fly well,

Rokugo tombi (paper hawk) kite by Nobuhiku Yoshizumi. Approx. 7.6 × 20.3 cm. Skinner Collection

Contemporary *tako-tako* (octopus kite) by Peter Lynn.
Showamachi Kite Museum

and the shape accommodates naturalistic depiction of creatures associated with flight—birds and insects—as well as broad-shouldered gods and human personages. There are numerous variations of this type of kite. In Japan these include *yakko* (footman/servant) kites, ever popular with young children; *tobi*, or its variant *tombi* (hawk) kites; and *sode* (sleeve) kites, modeled on the shape of the Japanese kimono. In China the T shape accommodates all kinds of birds as well as the Eight Immortals of Chinese mythology. Three factors—exemplary flight, ease of construction, and appropriateness for a variety of realistically rendered images—have enabled the T-shaped kite to hold its own alongside the basic rectangular kite as one of the more familiar and traditional Asian kite forms.

The first extant visual representation of a Japanese kite occurs in the *Wakan sansai zue*, an illustrated encyclopedia published in Japan in 1712. The Chinese characters and the translation in Japanese of *ika-nobori* (*ika*: octopus or squid; *nobori*: flag or banner) are accompanied by a drawing of a kite, flying line, and reel. The kite looks very much like an octopus, a form well suited to a kite. Five octopus-like "tentacles"—thin ribbons of paper that function (exceedingly well for the purposes of steady flight) as tails—are attached separately to the bell-like, octopus-shaped body. In the *Wakan sansai zue* illustration, the tentacles writhe realistically. It is a convincing abstraction of a live octopus. In daily life the *ika-nobori* kite often appeared as a sign outside kite shops, advertising wares within. The *ika* kite is still made in Japan, a memento in recognition of its early appearance in Japanese kite history.

To illustrate the often inherently confusing nature of translating Chinese characters into spoken Japanese, in the *Wakan sansai zue*, *ika* (squid), is given as the Japanese reading of the Chinese characters for *shien* (paper hawk). In modern times, while they still share the same Chinese character, the common word for kites in spoken Japanese is *tako*; in Mandarin, modern spoken Chinese, *fengzheng*. As Japanese love puns, perhaps it is no coincidence that in spoken Japanese, *tako* also means "octopus." Although the accepted translation of *fengzheng* is "kite," the elements that make up the two written characters can be translated as "wind harp." This is an allusion to tenth-century kites that carried bamboo pipes played by the wind; their sound resembled the *zheng*, a Chinese stringed instrument.

The *tobi* or *tombi*, the hawk kite mentioned as a popular version of the T-shaped kite, is named after the Japanese word for the Siberian black kite, *Milvus melanotis*. Compound words in Japanese beginning with *tobi* refer to different elements of flight: "up," "to soar high," "flying to and fro," for example.

The *tobi/tombi* hawk kite may have been a generic word for "kite" in some regions. Like *tako* and *ika*, *tobi* (up) and *tombi* (hawk) are examples of the pleasure the Japanese take in double meanings

"Bone" structure of a Hamamatsu kite.

and play on words. I should also mention that the color of the Siberian black kite notwithstanding, these Japanese paper-hawk kites are interpreted, in the various regions where the kite is made, not only in black, but in brown, gray, and red as well.

Characteristics of Chinese and Japanese Kites

Kitemakers in both China and Japan customarily use bamboo for the kite's framework. The strength, flexibility, and ready availability of bamboo are properties uniquely suited to kites. The bamboo framework of Chinese kites can be formidably complicated, because Chinese kites are more frequently three-dimensional. Japanese kite structures, by comparison, are generally relatively simple; with few exceptions they are flat and bowed to increase stability. Chinese kites tend to bear mimetic, representational images, while Japanese kite embellishments can be characterized as abstract, emblematic simplifications of nature. The covering of the highest grade of Chinese kite is silk; the less expensive, common Chinese kite is of paper. Although paper was invented in China, Japanese paper from the beginning has been far superior to its Chinese counterpart. Japan's traditional kites are made exclusively of *washi,* a handmade, exceptionally strong and durable paper. The traditional Japanese kite's decoration is characterized by the thick and thin brushstrokes of *sumi-e* (ink) painting, using techniques rooted in the dramatic flourishes of Japanese calligraphy. The draftsmanship in *tako-e* (kite art) differs markedly from the intricate tracery of fine, even lines familiar in Chinese kite painting. Japanese kites are distinguished by eye-catching, bold, evenly applied colors that produce an effect quite different from the light tints, lyrical pastels, and the shading techniques typical of traditional Chinese kite painting.

above: Images of kabuki actors depicted on kites. Detail of an *ukiyo-e*
woodblock print by Yoshiharu. 1864. Skinner Collection
left: A Beauty Spot in the Enshu District, featuring a Fukuroi kite. *Ukiyo-e* woodblock
print by Hiroshige Ando (1797–1858). Skinner Collection

By the eighteenth century, Japan had absorbed the Chinese kitemaking influence, and the distinctive Japanese kites recognized today came into their own, establishing uniquely Japanese outposts in the sky.

Kabuki and *Ukiyo-e* Kite Art

Among highly popular kites in the eighteenth century were those with images of kabuki theater characters that embraced the posterlike *ukiyo-e* woodblock-print colors and drawing style. Both kabuki and *ukiyo-e* prints (pictures of the "floating world") were well established by the time of the kite's emergence as one of Japan's popular art forms.

Kabuki theater dates from the end of the sixteenth century. Wildly popular, it was a must-see for citizens and visitors to the capital city of Edo, present-day Tokyo. The most frequented theater in Edo bore the name Kabuki-za. Built in 1660, it stands today and is as popular as ever.

Kite featuring Momotaro, the Peach Boy.
Shirone Kite Museum

Ukiyo-e woodblock prints date from the seventeenth century. Initially scenes of everyday life, these genre pictures were soon joined by the most glamorous images in popular Japanese culture—entertainers and historical and mythological figures.

Famous heroes and legendary characters depicted in the kabuki theater and in *ukiyo-e* prints were among the intrinsically Japanese images that distinguished Japanese kites from their Chinese counterparts. Edo visitors were apparently the initiators of the subject matter popular on Japanese traditional kites, subjects still popular to this day. From the beginning, kitemakers found it impossible to resist the demand for kites depicting kabuki characters in the *ukiyo-e* style. Although the grimacing warrior portraits and lavish attire we still see depicted on traditional Japanese kites appear to be highly stylized, they are in fact fairly realistic renditions of the elaborate make-up and extravagant clothing worn by kabuki actors. Kitemakers, it turns out, regularly attended kabuki performances for the sole purpose of studying these samurai characters in order to add them to their kite-painting repertoire.

In addition to subject matter, art and design qualities were a source of inspiration for kite art. *Nishiki-e* (brocade sash painting), a stock-in-trade of the Edo kitemaker, was based on a richly complex, detailed style of woodblock art. The bright colors and dramatic design qualities of *nishiki* and *ukiyo* art seemed perfectly suited to kites. The artistic element must have contributed its share to keeping the kitemakers' rice bowls full: business was good enough to support over one hundred kitemakers in eighteenth-century Edo alone.

Development of Regional Styles

A great many travelers passed through Edo in the eighteenth century. Provincial lords were required by law to make twice-yearly visits to the capital. When the lords and their retainers—entourages that could number in the hundreds—returned home bearing the requisite gifts for stay-at-homes, provincial kitemakers gained access to first-class models, which influenced their own kite work. (Innumerable *mingei*—people's art, or popular folk-art forms—profited, along with kites, from the imperatives of gift-giving.) At first imitating Edo kites, provincial designs gradually evolved into the distinctive regional kites—representing a village, town, prefecture, or district—that are known today across Japan.

Religion, Play, and Traditional Social Restraints

Prior to *ukiyo-e* kabuki models, the earliest kites in Japan were bound to religious beliefs. This early connotation remained until relatively modern times in modest ceremonies connected with daily life, such as planting and harvesting in the countryside. In farming communities, families still tie stalks of rice to their kites as a symbolic offering of thanks. Priests give their blessing to these kites as well as to kites celebrating the birth of male children. Kites can be purchased at temples and shrines as talismans against sickness and misfortune. Though there might still be residual pockets of belief in supernatural powers, by the late nineteenth or early twentieth century, these ceremonies and kites simply paid token honor to old customs; generally speaking, today they lack their earlier religious certitude.

The connection between boys and kites—exemplified by the tradition of giving kites to young boys and to families celebrating first-born sons—prevails in modern times. In a period when attention is being focused on equality of the sexes, however, traditions promoting gender-based participation are breaking down. In general, kite activities throughout Japan seem to be moving toward implementation of celebration and play available and enjoyable to both sexes. In the formerly all-male domain of kites, it is becoming common to see women and young girls flying and making kites.

In Japan at the end of the seventeenth century, kites were still associated with religion, but, as the kabuki kite souvenirs suggest, the profane, playful aspects of Japanese kites were already on the rise. The early eighteenth century in Japan was marked, in fact, by a kite mania. Western encyclopedias describe Japanese skies filled with kites; shopkeepers stood in their doorways neglecting business, oblivious to customers, completely engrossed in flying kites. Countless laws were enacted to enforce restraint, to stem play, and to point citizens in the direction of the propriety of purposeful pursuits. These included a plea for the time-honored tradition of maintaining appearances of frugality and refraining from excess of any kind. Among the many items restricted were lavishly and ostentatiously colored clothing and kites. Despite all efforts to subdue behavior deemed inappropriate, contemporary accounts noted that the people were not easily diverted from their unabashed love of kites; the kite mania continued to rage.

Characteristics of Japanese Kites: Giants and Miniatures

Regulating a kite's size was another high priority of Japanese lawmakers in earlier times. Kites had grown so large that they had become lethal weapons, capable of hurting people, damaging property, and destroying crops. But these perils as well as the laws prohibiting large kites apparently went unheeded by the kite-loving Japanese. They had long taken delight in seeing and experiencing things in their extremes, particularly in the matter of size. (This same fascination for extremes in scale can be found throughout Asia.) Kitemakers, responsive to their customers' demands, also commonly

Isao Ogawa with examples of his miniature *semi* (cicada) kites.

made tiny kites of 4 by 6 centimeters, sometimes smaller. Inasmuch as the professional kitemaker's work was measured by its flying ability, these miniatures were expected to fly. Anything incapable of flight was considered a compelling novelty. One could find kites for Lilliputians: tiny kites that balanced on the point of a pin, visible only with a magnifying lens. It is difficult to imagine such a minuscule object made of bamboo and paper—including a detailed painted decoration—but an example of just such a kite is on display at Tokyo's Japan Kite Museum.

Standard-size kites made by Japan's professional kitemakers are in the neighborhood of 1.5 to 3 meters square and approximately 0.3 to 2 meters high. Kites of 2 meters may have been the limit expected of a kitemaker working alone (not just because of the effort and the time involved; the expense of making large kites is considerable). The help and expertise of professionals is often called upon in the construction of much, much larger kites weighing thousands of pounds, as big as a house, and made and flown with community-wide participation. These are the extraordinary *odako*, giant kites that reached their apogee by the 1930s with the *wan wan* kite, made and flown in the town of Naruto, Tokushima prefecture. This mammoth oval-shaped kite lifted off the ground at 24 meters across at its widest dimension and a weight of 2,500 kilograms.

Kite Season in Japan

In Japan, as in the West, kite flying is a seasonal activity and celebrates the arrival of spring and warm weather. In Japan it is also associated with the beginning of the New Year in midwinter. This tradition does not correlate well with winter's realities of kite flying, since one must bundle up against the cold in much of Japan at this time of year. Flying a kite while wearing wool mittens is not, even for die-hard kite flyers, that much fun. Thus, while kites grace virtually every shop window in Tokyo during the month of January and may be found at certain shrines and offered for sale as seasonal New Year gifts at many department store *mingei* counters, few kites actually fly for any length of time in the cold winter months.

During the weeks around May 5 (formerly Boy's Day, now celebrated as Children's Day), the weather is a better complement to kite flying. From the beginning of May through the early summer months, kites make a strong presence as a popular activity for both adults and children.

Japanese Kites Entering the Twenty-First Century

Despite the enduring success of Japan's kite festivals, which grow year by year, like all Japanese traditional popular art forms, the traditional art of kitemaking had long faced an unsure future. Would these old art forms, and the artists lovingly holding on to the ancient traditions, survive in a rapidly modernizing Japan? Would the professional artist/craftsmen become an anachronistic embarrassment no longer relevant in Japan's modern society?

During the last quarter of this century Japan leapt into its modern age, becoming a world-class leader in the manufacture of high-end automobiles and consumer electronics. It soon added to its résumé the title of the world's number-one banker. The transformation of Tokyo's skyline into a wall of glass and steel skyscrapers left little doubt as to its economic preeminence. In a country which now claimed having the world's largest airline, it seemed inevitable that the old traditional paper and bamboo kites would surely disappear from Japan's skies. Why this did not happen, the persistence of tradition fulfilling some intangible need in a contemporary society, might be the basis of an interesting study.

The number of traditional professional kite artists has declined in modern times. Formerly, kitemakers hung on to their profession out of love or an ingrained sense of responsibility for fulfilling inherited roles. A family provider may have become the family's first kitemaker during the hard feudal times as a strategy for adding some grains to the rice bowl, but, in later years, a kitemaker's rice bowl tended to remain half full. Twentieth-century kitemakers were usually found among Japan's less advantaged poor. Approximately thirty-five traditional kite artists have survived. Their small number surely accounts for the general improvement in their financial status. Today's traditional kitemakers are hard-pressed to keep up with the demand for their kites, particularly at the height of kite season. It's still a demanding profession; one characterized by handwork, almost by definition unsuited to

Japan Kite Association member Terauki Tsutsumi teaching kitemaking in Shirone.

Teizo Hashimoto leading a kitemaking workshop in the late 1940s.

modernization, assembly lines, and mechanization. It is a profession on which the kitemakers' heirs have largely turned their backs in favor of salaried employment. The remaining professionals are thus revered by an appreciative community and garner attention and honors both in Japan and throughout the world as artists who give life and vibrancy to the thread connecting the riches of present-day Japan and its equally rich past.

The number of nonprofessional kitemakers has increased from none to thousands. Many contemporary amateurs begin their kitemaking careers in middle age while holding down jobs, then assume the role of full-time kitemaker upon retirement from their primary occupation. In days past, kitemaking was practiced almost exclusively by men. Today, more women are working as serious amateurs. And among the small number of professionals are a half-dozen highly regarded women who have taken the mantle from their fathers. In one instance, the Kato family in Shizuoka, makers of the traditional Suruga kite, there are now three generations of women kitemakers.

The distinction between "amateur" and "professional" in Japan (a similar distinction is maintained in China) has no connotation other than that the professionals' status protects their livelihood. Amateurs have all the rights of kitemaking and festival participation, and may be equal if not superior in talent, but they are not allowed to compete with a professional's income from sales. In effect, a professional's identification with a regional kite is interpreted as a copyright protecting the maker's rights as they pertain to the sale of this kite.

The New Japanese Kite

Adding to the numbers of talented, serious amateurs and professionals, Japanese kite enthusiasts have recently begun making their own kites. They find guidance in workshops and from a host of popular how-to kitemaking books available in Japan's bookstores.

Currently holding the record as author of the most books in print on this subject is Eiji Ohashi, a modern kite inventor, eminent kite flyer, and regional festival organizer in the Tokyo region. Along with Masaaki Modegi and Takeshi Nishibayashi (see pp. 76–77), Ohashi is one of Japan's most widely traveled international kite festival participants. Known for his long, long ribbons of kite "trains," Ohashi has flown his kites literally almost around the world and spends weeks and months at a time in cities East and West as a kind of kite goodwill ambassador, attracting countless thousands to the pleasures of kitemaking in his workshops and kite-flying spectacles.

Japan's kitemaking workshops are held in December and during April and May. Tsutomu Hiroi, a multitalented sculptor, kitemaker, university professor, and practicing industrial designer who has worked on projects alongside Japanese-American sculptor Isamu Noguchi, is often cited as the dean of this novel workshop idea. Hiroi is also the author of widely popular books on Japanese kites, which include modern Western models—also featured in his workshops—and which helped foster the awareness that new kite forms could emerge not just out of the West but from Japan as well. A quite novel idea, workshops may have helped set in motion the dramatic change in the Japanese attitude which, until then, constantly reinforced the notion that only professional Japanese kitemakers could be responsible for making traditional Japanese kites. Eiji Ohashi, formerly a textbook publishing house editor, was one such "amateur" whose first exposure to kitemaking came while accompanying his son to a Hiroi kite workshop in Tokyo.

For many Japanese, these first experiences in making their own kites led to appreciation and serious commitment. This is not just tied to people at the retirement age: kite festivals and clubs are filled with a full spectrum of ages and people from all walks of life. Eventually Japan's professionals, the kitemakers who had inherited their kitemaking mantles through family lines, became enthusiastic supporters of kitemaking workshops. With their children choosing other work, the traditional kitemakers revealed some of their long-held family secrets to school children and adults as well, knowing in their hearts that this openness would contribute to the continued good health and future life of kites in Japan. This new openness also signaled a frank appreciation of good fun, free of the formality and inhibiting restraints of an older social order. It resulted in a profusion of new appealing and endlessly fascinating varieties of kites soaring in Japan's skies. It is gratifying to observe that many of these new kitemakers have earned recognition for their kite artistry both within and outside Japan.

Today, kites have their role among the tools of science and technology. In the West, kites are continually being reexamined for new applications. Modern kite inventions have found a home in the space program in the form of a huge kite moving in space via solar winds, and closer to earth they are employed as tools of upper atmospheric research. Closer still, they are used in mapping and aerial photography. There is a Western association whose members are dedicated to exploring the use of modern kites and developing related equipment for aerial photography. This organization has its counterpart in Japan. Its president, the kitemaker, artist, and inventor Katsutaka Murooka (see pp. 74–75), is represented by popular books illustrating his work as well as by technical treatises describing the evaluative methodology this young man, another gifted, multitalented Japanese kitemaker, has developed.

Participation in the Worldwide Kite Community

In a relatively recent development, a number of Japanese communities have undertaken bold initiatives, calling attention to their region's involvement with kites. Participation and local support for these new community kite museums functions at a truly astonishing level. Kite-preservation societies in Hamamatsu, Ikazaki, Shirone, Showamachi, Tokyo, and Yokaichi (to name some of the most prominent) have inspired and assisted in the realization of major commitments to kites. Ultramodern public museums dedicated to the exhibition of kite collections and local kite archives celebrate the history and contemporary life and role of kites in their communities. The Shirone Kite Museum, dedicated in 1994, is a handsome four-story glass and concrete city landmark with an amazing 27,000 square feet of exhibition space. (See Appendix B: Kite Museums with Japanese Kite Collections for additional information.)

The Japanese have also been generous in exporting their kite enthusiasm. In recent times Japan's kite flyers, in conjunction with the Japan Kite Association, have participated in kite festivals on every continent. These men and women kite flyers bring to festival skies around the world marvelous new kite inventions incorporating state-of-the art materials as well as examples of their country's traditional kites. For thousands of international kite enthusiasts, Japanese kites represent at once the newest and the oldest, and at their best, the finest, most engaging sky-art form being produced anywhere in the world.

Preparing to launch a Machijirushi kite in Hamamatsu.

A Precursor and Model for Modern Works of Fine Art

The art at the heart of what we might perceive as Japan's humble, play-oriented kite is quite remarkable. Elements of Japanese kite art have even contributed to the development of art in the West. Art historians have long acknowledged the influence of *ukiyo-e* prints, the staple of Japanese kite art, on European and American artists of the nineteenth century—Henri de Toulouse-Lautrec, Vincent van Gogh, Edgar Degas, Mary Cassatt, and James Abbott McNeill Whistler—as well as on many twentieth-century masters.

Present-day Western artists who became acquainted with Edo master kitemaker Teizo Hashimoto's magnificent kite paintings through books have acknowledged respect for his kite art and have dedicated exhibitions of their work to his memory. Many art cognoscenti who applaud the work of American sculptor Kenneth Snelson are also familiar with his bamboo sculptures—variations on his innovative tensegrity, tension/compression stainless-steel sculptures—which, he acknowledges, refer to traditional Asian bamboo kite frames.

"Kite art" in a Japanese kitemaker's lexicon is not just the painting on the kite's surface but the whole kite seen as a kinetic object: the kite in flight. Most of Japan's kitemakers respond to the question of what they consider the most important aspect of their art not by drawing attention to their kite's painting or their skills as craftsmen (which are self-evident), but by stating unequivocally that the kite must, above all, fly well. Its special beauty is implicit in its function. In this respect Japanese kites in flight can be appreciated as models for the modernist movements—kinetic art, environmental art, temporal art, happenings, and performance art and events—and, certainly, the most inclusive modernist movement to embrace kites, sky art. The influence of old kites and kite flying on contemporary art, conveyed through books, exhibitions, and kite festivals, continues to inspire artists, East and West.

The Element of Play in Contemporary Art

The Dutch philosopher Johan Huizinga in his book *Homo Ludens, a Study of the Play Element in Culture* (New York: Roy Publishers, 1949) theorized that art was a game played according to rules that are forever changing in the course of history but which, nonetheless, create a situation wherein the condition of humankind's meaninglessness becomes meaningful, and as adults, we can learn to play and love all over again. It is not a comfortable thought for those who require the imprimatur of seriousness—a tragic, guilt-edged view opposed to the comedic spirit, we might say—to extol human endeavors. American sculptor Alexander Calder's lighthearted playfulness was a highly contentious issue throughout his career. Calder, oriented to deflating pomposity, refused to give up fun and cheery good humor. The underlying concept of his mobile inventions, so much in tune with the blithe spirit of kites, kite art, and kite flying, drew its inspiration from a larger arena. "Playing field" is an apt description, already well explored and defined by kites. Reading Calder's characterization of his mobiles, I can't help but marvel at the nearly identical condition of kites and the typical appearance of kites at a festival:

> The underlying sense of form in my work has been the system of the Universe. . . . The idea of detached bodies floating in space, of different sizes and densities, perhaps of different colors . . . seems to me the ideal source of form. I would have them deployed, some nearer together and some at immense distances. And great disparity among all the qualities of these bodies, and their motions as well. . . . For the object floating—not supported—the use of a very long thread, or a long arm in cantilever as means of support seems to best approximate this freedom from the earth.[1]

Lightness and Weight

What more can we say about the special character and pleasure inherent in kites, shared universally by people of all ages and all nations?

Author Italo Calvino, in the opening sentences of his brilliant essays on literature, written for Harvard's Norton Lectures, announced his desire to elude "the weight, the inertia, the opacity of the world . . . the entire world . . . turning into stone" in favor of "the quick light touch I wanted for my writing." He went on to say:

> Whenever humanity seems condemned to heaviness, I think I should fly like Perseus into a different space. I don't mean escaping into dreams or into the irrational. I mean that I have to change my approach, look at the world from a different perspective, with a different logic and with fresh methods of cognition and verification. The images of lightness that I seek should not fade away like dreams dissolved by the realities of present and future.[2]

The lightness of kites, the joy that accompanies the lifting of psychological weight as you enter into this world of kites, is a wonder. Children intuitively understand and appreciate all of this in all the important ways. But deep within older psyches also resides the ability to enter and revel in this experience. The proof lies in the exponential increase in adult participants, in what might be described as a kite explosion, not just in Japan but worldwide.

For Japanese men, women, and children, that unique and universal pleasure, the kite smile, is just a heartbeat away. Surely no more profound nor joyful expression of this pleasure may be found than in Japan. In a rapidly shrinking world of crosscultural fertilization, the recognition of the unique quality of Japanese kites, already high, is sure to grow even higher. You can confirm it yourself—just look up to enjoy Japan's high art!

NOTES

1. Alexander Calder, "What Abstract Art Means to Me," *Museum of Modern Art Bulletin* 3: XVIII (1951): 8.

2. Italo Calvino, *Six Memos for the Next Millennium* (Cambridge, Mass: Harvard University Press, 1988), pp. 4, 7.

pages 28–29: Cartoon of a Shirone kite battle printed on *hachimaki* (headbands).

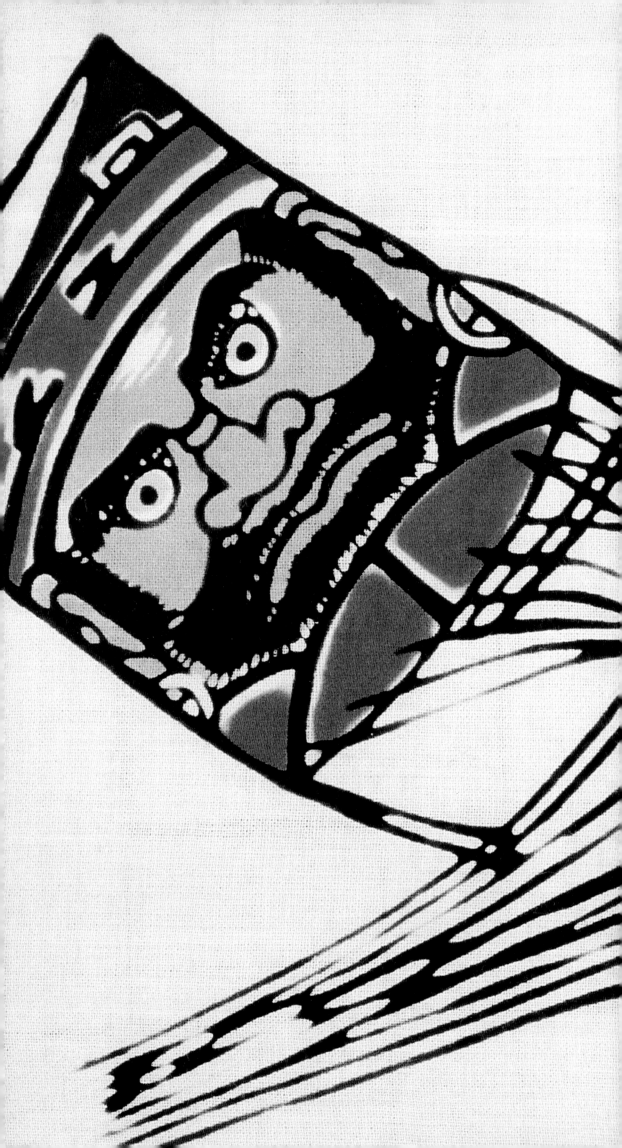

Anatomy of a Kite

Scott Skinner

Bamboo, Paper, Paint

Bamboo

In North America, I think it is safe to say that bamboo is intimidating to most modern kitemakers. We are more comfortable using carbon-fiber or fiberglass spars with ripstop nylon sail covers that can be sewn around the frames. Yet it is undeniable that bamboo is the most versatile framing material, and it is the one found in most traditional Japanese kites. Remarkably strong, yet lightweight and flexible, it is a completely controllable sparring material. It can be tapered to control flex, can be bent and formed to any shape, and can be used in thicknesses from several inches to only millimeters.

It is fascinating to realize that material split from a single bamboo pole might be used in a Shirone giant kite, in a delicate miniature the size of an actual insect, or in kites of any size in between. Japanese bamboo (fig. 1) is normally harvested between November and January to avoid insect infestation of the warmer seasons. Best split when green, it is easier to work than dried bamboo. Yet many kitemasters in Japan prefer to demonstrate their skill by using very old, well-dried bamboo. This material is salvaged from traditional houses being torn down for new development. Besides being beautiful to look at—aged bamboo often has a smoky brown patina from years of cooking smoke—it is extremely light and strong. Bamboo used for everyday kites is often dried and stored for two years or more.

There are many techniques for working bamboo and, in many cases, the specific type of bamboo may dictate the technique. In general, however, the kite bamboo of Japan is of good quality, and the following techniques do well for working it. Bamboo is cut to workable lengths with a hacksaw or Japanese bamboo saw. Bamboo splits easily lengthwise and should be worked in equal sizes (the same amount of bamboo on either side of the split). Starting with a full bamboo stem, or a stem of the length you desire, split the entire length in half, then split this pair in half, and continue until you have widths for your particular use. Most who are adept at splitting bamboo use a thick-bladed bamboo knife (fig. 2) that really works as a wedge, not as a cutting tool. The crack created by this knife can be driven or controlled by blade pressure on either side of the piece being split. Care must be taken when driving the crack through the knots—this is one place where there is no substitute for practice, though shaving down the excess material behind the knot can help.

Split lengths of bamboo can be tapered or their rigidity adjusted by shaving the back (cortex) of the spar. The skin contains most of the spar's strength, but loss of all strength results if the cortex is shaved to nothing. There is a trade-off here: in considering the kite's overall weight, the cortex is the heaviest material, but it also is necessary for overall strength. You must

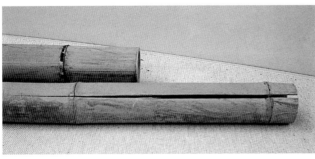

fig. 1

fig. 2

fig. 3   fig. 4

decide how much to shave off for your particular use. One trick that I have seen employed in both China and Japan ensures symmetry of any two pieces in a particular kite: a double-width piece of bamboo is first shaped or shaven to a desired thickness and afterward split down the middle, giving the kitemaker two equal spars for the opposite sides of the kite. Symmetry of cross sticks or "bow" sticks, like those in Nagasaki fighters (fig. 3), is best done by bending from both ends and observing inconsistencies of the curve. Sometimes pieces need to be bent permanently. Bamboo can be bent by slowly heating the area where the bend is needed over a flame or other heat source and then slowly bending it as it begins to brown. To set the bend, it must be cooled quickly in water or with a wet cloth.

Some kites from particular regions of Japan do not use bamboo spars. Examples include the bird kites of Niigata, which use reed, and the Tsugaru kites of northern Japan (fig. 4), which use *hiba*, or cypress.

Paper

Most traditional Japanese kites are made with *washi* paper, which is hand made from fibers extracted from *kozo* or *mitsumata* plants (mulberry, and *Edgeworthia chrysanthe*). *Washi* is made to be incredibly strong by overlapping its long, soft fibers in vertical and horizontal layers. Most Western papers tear easily because they are made from wood pulp, with relatively short, hard fibers.

Contemporary kitemakers have substituted a variety of materials for their kites, including poly-

ethylene (fig. 5), Tyvek®, vinyl sheeting, and ripstop nylon. Most notably, Tyvek®, by DuPont, is used increasingly in large kites because it is more durable and weatherproof than paper, but traditional festivals that feature large kites (as do Hamamatsu, Sagamihara, and Shirone) continue to use *washi*.

Paint

Most kite artists use dry color pigments mixed with water (although Tsutomu Hiroi notes elsewhere that they are often mixed with slight amounts of alum and glue) that produce brilliant, vivid color. Because the paint tends to rapidly bleed into the paper, a *sumi-e* (ink painting) or *hanga* (woodblock print) is often done first, or, alternatively, a wax outline is applied to define the design. Either technique restricts the color to the desired areas.

fig. 5

Aerodynamics

In general, three aerodynamic forces act upon a kite in flight: lift, drag, and gravity. For the sake of study, we assume that these forces act upon a single point on a kite's surface. The center of lift is that point at which the air pressure against the kite's surface is concentrated; center of drag is the point at which all the resistant forces of the airflow are concentrated; and center of gravity occurs where all the weight of the kite is concentrated. All three forces are balanced at the center of pressure, and ideally, the kite line and towing point align through the kite's center of pressure (fig. 1). This determines the kite's attitude in flight.

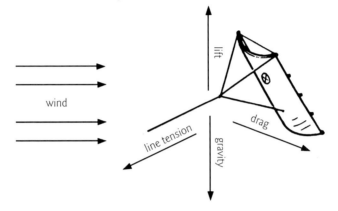

fig 1. The three aerodynamic forces: lift, drag, and gravity,
with the center of pressure denoted by "⊗".

Aspect ratio is the relationship of the width of the kite to its length. In most cases, the flat, geometric kites of Japan have relatively low aspect ratios (fig. 2). They are very stable, fly in heavier winds, and have a high sink rate in low winds. Higher aspect ratio kites, like the Niigata bird kites or the Tokyo *tombi* (fig. 3), are less stable but fly remarkably well in low winds.

TSUGARU KITE

TOMBI KITE

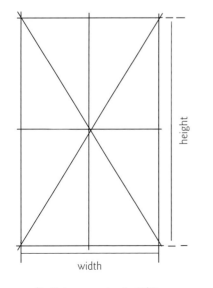

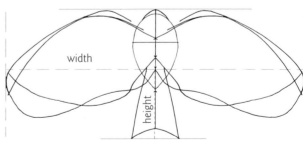

fig. 3. High aspect ratio (2/1); wing span is
2 units to every unit of body length.

fig. 2. Low aspect ratio (2/3);
stable flyer; flies in heavier winds.

Lateral stability—the ability to maintain straight-ahead flight—is greatly enhanced through the use of dihedral (bow) (fig. 4), but in many of the flat kites of Japan, it is augmented by the use of tails (fig. 5). Vertical surfaces like those on a box kite can also contribute to lateral stability but are rare in traditional Japanese kites.

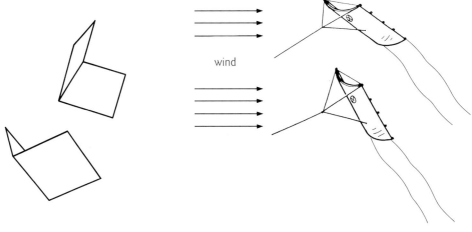

wind

<table>
<tr><td>fig. 4. Dihedral, the angle of the wings, or the bow of a kite.</td><td>fig. 5. Kites showing dihedral (bow) and further stablized by the use of tails.</td></tr>
</table>

How a Fighter Kite Flies

The Nagasaki *hata* is a very good example of a maneuverable, single-line fighting kite. Flown with a glass-coated line, the darting kite is made to cut the line of an opponent. A flat, tailless kite, the *hata* is inherently unstable (fig. 6); it can yaw, slip, or even roll if the kite flyer does nothing to control it. Control is achieved by pulling on the kite line; the resultant pressure on the surface of the kite causes it to flex back (fig. 7). The flex in the kite's wings causes dihedral, and the dihedral provides momentary directional stability. As long as the kite flyer maintains tension on the line, the kite will fly in a straight track. Releasing that tension causes the kite to flatten, stop, and spin until pressure is reapplied when the kite is facing the desired direction (fig. 8).

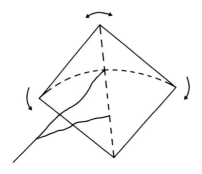

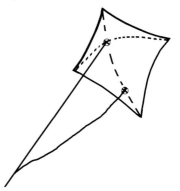

fig. 6. A flat kite is inherently unstable.

fig. 7. Tension applied on the kite line causes the kite to flex back. The flex causes dihedral, and dihedral provides momentary directional stability.

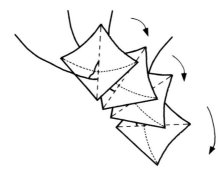

fig. 8. Slackening of the line causes the kite to stop and spin.

The Kitemaker's Measure

Kitemakers from any part of the world are familiar with the modular approach to kite building. Wings are built to a certain length to avoid wasting fabric or dowels. The finished kite is constructed to be transported easily. The same is true in the Japanese kitemaking tradition. The standard unit of measure is not meters, or feet and inches, however, but the traditional tatami mat, whose dimensions also define floor area of the traditional Japanese house. This unit, approximately 95 by 190 cm, is frequently used when referring to either a standard or a giant kite's size. The famous Hoshubana Giant, for instance, measured 100 tatami mats, or 19 by 14 meters.

Another unit of measure important to the kitemaker is the size of one sheet of *washi* paper. To minimize waste, the kite builder adopts the standard *washi* sheet (about 33 by 48 cm) and constructs the kite in terms of its proportions. For example, a large *Edo-dako* made by Teizo Hashimoto was constructed from eight sheets of paper arranged in an offset pattern to avoid long, weak seam lines. The kite measures approximately 132 cm high and 96 cm wide.

Contemporary kitemakers have adopted new materials such as ripstop nylon and Tyvek® for their creations. The manufacturing modules of these materials do not, of course, have any relationship with traditional sizes or modules for kite building. With these modern materials, kitemakers have also implemented new dimensions in their works.

above: A large Shirone-style kite ready for launch on the beach at Uchinada.
right: Old and new: A giant kite made of bamboo and Tyvek®.

Regional Forms

Kites in Japan have developed regionally or locally, and it is not uncommon for two cities within a very small area to have completely different kite traditions. Geography greatly influences the kites of each region. Areas with higher winds require kites with stronger structures; lack or abundance of bamboo dictates structural material. Regional kite styles are shown in many *ukiyo-e* prints from the 1800s: not only are those styles of kites still being produced, but their artwork is as well.

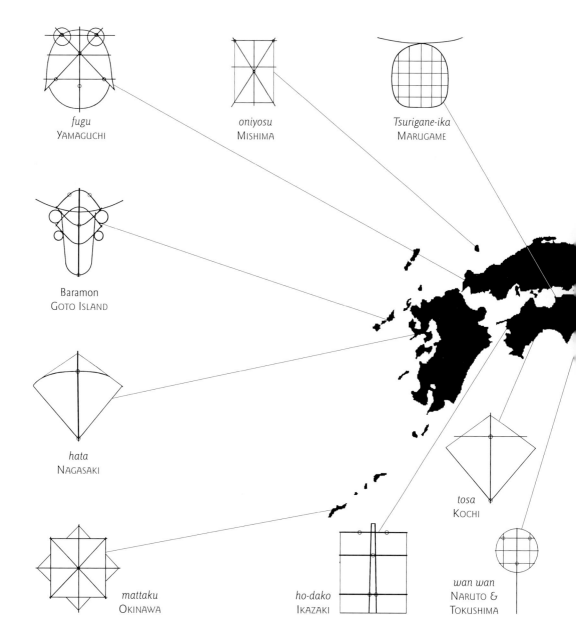

fugu
YAMAGUCHI

oniyosu
MISHIMA

Tsurigane-ika
MARUGAME

Baramon
GOTO ISLAND

hata
NAGASAKI

tosa
KOCHI

mattaku
OKINAWA

ho-dako
IKAZAKI

wan wan
NARUTO &
TOKUSHIMA

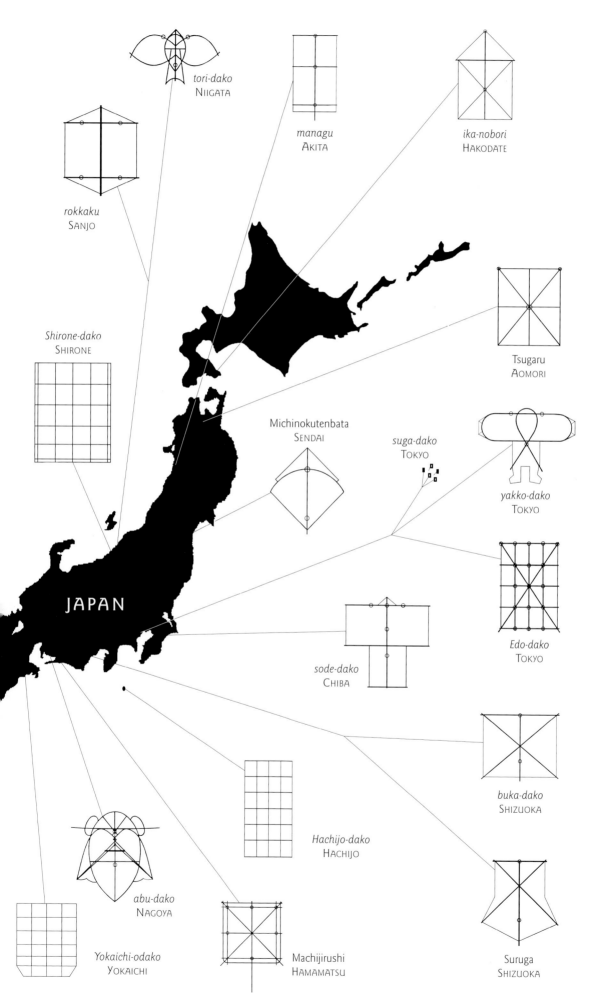

tori-dako
NIIGATA

managu
AKITA

ika-nobori
HAKODATE

rokkaku
SANJO

Shirone-dako
SHIRONE

Tsugaru
AOMORI

Michinokutenbata
SENDAI

suga-dako
TOKYO

yakko-dako
TOKYO

JAPAN

sode-dako
CHIBA

Edo-dako
TOKYO

buka-dako
SHIZUOKA

abu-dako
NAGOYA

Hachijo-dako
HACHIJO

Yokaichi-odako
YOKAICHI

Machijirushi
HAMAMATSU

Suruga
SHIZUOKA

Kite Art and Folklore

We are struck by the bold motifs, vibrant colors, and fine detail of Japanese kite art. Famous characters from Japanese folklore, kabuki theater, or military history are common motifs and may be found on almost every style of kite. Since kite flying was a traditional activity on Boy's Day (now Children's Day), it is natural to see images of Kintaro, hero of young boys, or, of *koi*—the carp, known for its strength and perseverance. The Seven Gods of Happiness, Daruma, and Okame, are examples of mystical or godlike characters who often find their way onto kites, and the dragon, at home in the clouds of mythology, is equally at home on a kite. Bold kanji ideographs are also seen frequently; these flying billboards may celebrate a new birth, "shout" a favorite phrase, or simply proclaim the owner of the kite. The following characters and motifs may appear on Japanese kites. Here, briefly, are their stories.

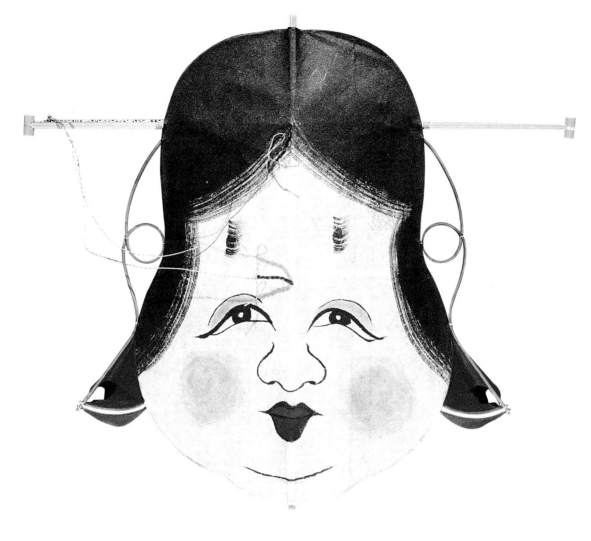

Okame

Okame is the Shinto goddess of mirth and sensuality (her full name is Ame no Uzume no Mikoto), and she is always shown with a smiling face, puffy cheeks, and a tiny mouth. Usually she has a narrow forehead with two ornamental black spots, and appears with her hair arranged in two bands over the temples. Appearing in Noh dramas and many Japanese arts, Okame is known to perform provocative dances in which she displays her more than ample charms. Statues and figures of the goddess represent her with various implements—reeds, *gohei*, or jingling bells bound around a stick or an arrow, an allusion to her famous dance in front of the cave from which the Dai Kagura—a series of sacred dances, performed at shrines on certain festivals by young female attendants—is said to be derived.

It is said that Amaterasu, the sun goddess, decided to hide in a cave after being insulted by her brother, the storm god. She closed the mouth of the cave with a giant boulder, casting the earth into darkness. To lure her back out, a huge mirror was forged, and a string of five hundred pearls was hung outside the cave. Okame came and began a particularly sensual dance, but the assembled deities burst into laughter at her comical figure. Hearing these noises, the sun goddess poked her head out of the cave to see what was happening and, seeing her image in the mirror, she emerged farther. The giant boulder was then rolled back into place behind her, and Amaterasu was forced to return to the world. Okame is thus credited with returning daylight to the world.

Okame is often treated humorously, scantily clad with bowed legs, or in a prettier mood as a comely girl casting dried peas at the devils in the Oni Yarai ceremony (wherein devils, or *oni*, are cast out of houses with the invocation, "Devils go away, Luck enter").

Okame's face is often seen on *Edo-dako* or Tsugaru kites but is most beautifully done in a *semi-dako* style of kite, with her face as the kite itself.

Okame kite in the style of *abu-*, *semi-*, or *hachi-dako* of Nagoya,
by Masaaki Sato. Skinner Collection

Detail of a kite by Imai. Shirone Kite Museum

Daruma

Daruma is the Japanese name for Bodhidharma, the sage who introduced the Zen sect of Buddhism to China. He is said to have left his teacher and retired in A.D. 520 to Lo Yang, where for nine years he remained seated, absorbed in meditation. Indifferent to temptations heaped upon him by evil spirits, often surrounded by demons of both sexes, or bitten on the ear or elsewhere by rats, at the end of this period Bodhidharma's legs had rotted away under him. This period is treated humorously by artists, and he is shown in a variety of ways.

Netsuke carvers often show him stretching himself or, more often, without legs, entirely enveloped in his red, baglike garments, showing his swarthy, scowling face. He is often found as a toy, usually with one eye open and one eye shut, and humorous prints show the toy coming to life when the eyes are marked out—an allusion to the popular belief that images of holy personages become alive when their "eyes are opened" by the priests. The *Tsurigane-ika* from Marugame is a kite built around the sitting form of Daruma. His image appears on kites from almost every region of Japan.

top: Yakko kite by Teizo Hashimoto. Checkley Collection, World Kite Museum
bottom: Tsurigane-ika kite by unknown maker. Shirone Kite Museum

Edo kite by Teizo Hashimoto. The Tokyo Kite Museum

Seven Gods of Good Fortune

The Shichi Fufujin, or Seven Gods of Good Fortune, are a favorite theme of the Japanese artist. They are almost always treated with rollicking good humor. Fukurokuju, with a very long head, is attended by a crane, deer, or tortoise; Daikoku stands upon rice bales and is accompanied by a rat; Ebisu carries a fish; Hotei is the embodiment of the phrase "laugh and grow fat." Benten, the only female of the group, is the goddess of beauty, wealth, fertility, and offspring; Bishamonten is armored and bears a spear and toy pagoda; and Jurojin is much like Fukurokuju.

The Seven Gods of Good Fortune are often shown as jovial passengers on the *Takarabune*, or Treasure Ship. At left, Teizo Hashimoto has masterfully shown them on a large *Edo-dako*. The *Takarabune* is said to come to port on New Year's Eve with no less a cargo than the Hat of Invisibility, the Lucky Raincoat (a protection from evil spirits), the Sacred Keys, the Inexhaustible Purse, Rolls of Brocade, and other curious and magical treasures known as the *takaramono*. Lucky dreams are said to come to children who place a picture of the treasure ship under their pillows.

Hotei is shown in all manner of Japanese arts and crafts and from his frequency must be the most popular of the Seven Gods of Good Fortune. He is almost always shown absurdly fat, joyously laughing, often accompanied by many children. His name is derived from the large linen bag he carries, in which he stores his precious things *(takaramono)* or which he uses as a receptacle for playful children.

In arts and children's dolls, Hotei smiles broadly. His protruding, naked abdomen represents largeness of soul, and his long earlobes symbolize wisdom and spiritual wealth. His sagging garments are a symbol of contentment and good nature. The flat, Chinese-style fan he often is shown carrying may refer to his Buddhist character. Hotei is always willing to do acts of kindness for others, and in Hotei's eyes, children can do no wrong. In old books, an easy way of drawing Hotei is shown: the outline of the character *kokoro* (心) forms his head, arms, neck, and abdomen.

Benten is the only female member of the Seven Gods of Good Fortune. She is the goddess of music, eloquence, arts, and fortune.

Daikoku is said to be the father of another of these seven gods, Ebisu. Daikoku is supposed to be the great bringer of luck. Usually represented as a fat, prosperous-looking individual, he wears a peculiar hat and often is depicted standing on two rice bales. He carries a hammer in his right hand, and, like Hotei, is often shown with a sack of precious things on his back.

Ebisu is the god of honest dealing, patron of fishermen, and the god of food. Legend has it that Ebisu started the custom of clapping hands before Shinto shrines in order to call the attention of the gods to the prayers being offered. Usually Ebisu is represented as a bearded, smiling man wearing a cap with two points and holding a fishing rod in one hand and a large tai fish in the other.

Both Jurojin and Fukurokuju are often pictured as a scholarly-looking old man with a snow-white beard. Jurojin has the attribute of longevity. Carrying a long staff with a scroll attached, he is also often accompanied by a crane, a stag, or a tortoise. Fukurokuju also typifies longevity and wisdom.

Bishamonten is the god of riches and one of the four Buddhist kings of heaven.

Yakko

The *yakko-odori*, or servants' dance, was an improvised dance practiced during the Genroku era (1688–1704). It poked fun at the self-important antics of the *yakko*, or footman, who was the lowest-ranking retainer of a feudal lord. Assigned to the menial tasks of the household, this didn't stop the *yakko* from bullying any commoners he encountered. One of this lowly servant's jobs was to clear commoners out of his master's way during travels.

Typical *yakko-dako* are in the shape and character of the footman: head bowed, *hapi* coat over bare chest, and fringed shorts over bare legs. Often the *yakko* kite has diamond motifs on both wings (symbols of the family), red and white skin, sword, and flapping legs. It is a kite typical of the Tokyo area and is seen in many *ukiyo-e* prints of the nineteenth century.

The *yakko-odori* is still performed in geisha houses, and one reason for the development of the kite is its natural dance on the wind, mimicking the *yakko-odori* of kabuki fame. The kite form can be adapted to depict birds or other human forms.

Kite flying and card games are New Year's pastimes, and simple *yakko* kites are sold at the Oji Inari Shrine in Tokyo at that time. Flying the kite ensures that it will clear the way to a happy and fire-free year. Kept indoors, it is believed the kite will protect the home against fire, and the kanji character representing fire (火) often adorns the *yakko* image's clothing, usually on his short pants.

Yakko kite by Teizo Hashimoto. Checkley Collection, World Kite Museum

Kintaro

Kintaro is a popular figure in Japanese art and on Japanese kites. Often called the Golden Boy, he is a child of the forest and possesses great strength. He is often shown wrestling with the beasts and goblins, including the monkey, stag, bear, and *tengu,* a mountain spirit. On children's kites he may appear carrying an enormous ax or wrestling with a great carp.

Kintaro was born on remote Ashigara Mountain, the son of Yaegiri and the disgraced officer Sakata Kurando. When only a few years old, Kintaro's mother gave him an ax, and he was able to fell trees with the strength and ease of an experienced woodcutter. Ashigara Mountain was a lonely spot, and he made companions of the bear, deer, hare, and monkey and was able to speak with them all. Upon hearing of the tragic death of Kintaro's father, Yorimitsu went to Yaegiri to ask if she would give him her child as a retainer. The Golden Boy followed Yorimitsu and was renamed Sakata Kintoki.

Children regard Kintaro as their favorite hero and emulate his strength and bravery. He is a favorite Children's Day doll and is usually depicted as a ruddy, half-clad child. He often wears a *haragake,* a small child's dress, and a lacquered court cap, sign of an aristocratic birth. He can be confused with another strong child, Momotaro, the Peach Boy. Under the name of Kimbei, he is the hero of the drama *Kimbei kashima maeri.*

Like Daruma, Kintaro may appear on kites from any region of Japan. He is also often shown on *koi no bori,* riding the largest carp, an image that celebrates the strength of a family's young boy.

Kintaro painted in the Tsugaru style, by unknown maker. Skinner Collection

Signs of the Zodiac (Juni-shi)

Usually found on children's kites or kites made especially for souvenirs, the twelve animals of the zodiac are commonly found on kites. They are: *ne*, the rat; *ushi*, the ox; *tora*, the tiger; *u*, the hare; *tatsu*, the dragon; *mi*, the snake; *uma*, the horse; *hitsuji*, the sheep; *saru*, the monkey; *tori*, the cock; *inu*, the dog; and *i*, the wild boar.

The Dragon

Of all the creatures forming the mythical fauna of Japanese lore, none is more often found in artwork than the dragon. Imported from the myths and legends of China, the Japanese dragon differs only in that it has three claws, unlike the Chinese dragon's five. The dragon has remarkable powers; if one ever sees its body in its entirety, death comes instantly. The Chinese emperor Yao was said to be the son of the dragon, as was the emperor of Japan. As such, he was hidden by bamboo curtains from the gaze of persons to whom he granted audiences, thus saving them from the terrible fate.

Tatsu the dragon is one of the signs of the zodiac, and the four seas (the Chinese limits of the habitable earth) are ruled by four dragon kings. The celestial dragon presides over the mansions of the gods, the spiritual dragon ministers to the rain, the earth dragon marks out the courses of rivers, and the dragon of hidden treasures watches over the precious metals and stones buried in the earth.

Dragon-form kites are famous in China, but in Japan the dragon is usually a motif to be used on any kite style.

Edo kite by Teizo Hashimoto. The Tokyo Kite Museum

Nami usagi

One of the most beautiful and endearing motifs to be found in Japanese art is the *nami usagi,* the rabbit and the wave. Rabbit legends and fables are plentiful, and the association to the hare and the moon is well known in Eastern art. In Japan, the hare has remained a lovable creature and is still associated with the moon. Does the image hearken back to a Buddhist legend of a hare given the privilege of living in the moon for his act of self-sacrifice? Or is the moon a symbol of *mochi,* the special confection that the rabbit is said to make with a mortar and pestle? Either way, the hare has become a symbol of good fortune. According to another legend, the female hare conceives by running on the waves on the eighteenth day of the eighth moon.

  The contrast of the design is engaging: the light and dark blue of the waves enhances the white of the hare. The hare is the embodiment of speed and motion: feet kicking, body tense and alert, it is cunning and its speed is obvious.

Edo kite by Teizo Hashimoto. The Tokyo Kite Museum

Shoki the Demon-Queller

Shoki, shown with flowing black beard and angular hat, is a mythical figure developed from Chinese stories. Said to be a guardian of the Emperor Genso, he had failed the imperial examinations and chose suicide rather than live with the shame of failure. Hearing of Shoki's honorable death, the emperor commanded that he be buried with full honors. In gratitude, Shoki's spirit vowed to remain in China forever, working to expel its demons.

The Japanese chose to picture him in military clothing, sword at the ready, hunting down *oni*—impish creatures that inhabit the forests. In contrast to his serious duty, Shoki is usually shown in humorous situations, often the victim of an *oni*'s tricks. The *oni* grin at Shoki and torment him by hiding throughout the countryside—they are so bold that they even hide under his hat.

Detail of a *rokkaku* kite by Mr. Sudo. Checkley Collection, World Kite Museum

Fujin

Fujin, the Japanese god of wind, is a green apparition that looks much like Hanya (see p. 50) or other *oni*. He is usually shown dashing across the sky with his large bag—inflated by the wind—draped over his shoulders. The character is often seen with Rainen, the god of thunder, on statuary, tapestry, *hapi* coats, and kites. Fujin is one of the symbols of the Japan Kite Association, so is seen frequently on contemporary kites.

Children's Edo kite by Teizo Hashimoto. Skinner Collection

Hanya

This sinister and scary female demon is often depicted on children's kites, *ko-dako*. Her blue face and horns are easily recognizable, and her image is said to frighten away evil spirits. Artists designing *ko-dako* made them inexpensive enough for common people to afford them and be able to dispose of them.

top: Edo kite by Teizo Hashimoto. Checkley Collection, World Kite Museum
bottom: Detail of a celebration kite from Yamagata prefecture,
by unknown maker. Skinner Collection

Watanabe no Tsuna

Watanabe was one of the retainers of the famous warrior Raiko (Minamoto no Yorimitsu). Raiko was famous for his energetic war on the many goblins and demons in Japan. When it was thought all were finally defeated, word came that one fearsome demon remained. It could be found living at Kyoto's Rashomon Gate, the entrance to the bridge across the Kamo River, which runs through the city. It was said that none dared spend the night there in order to kill it. Watanabe took up the challenge and, fighting sleep, waited through bad weather for the *oni* to appear.

As morning approached, sleep was finally overtaking Watanabe. Feeling a tug on his helmet, he collected himself and slashed at a dark mass over the gate. A piercing scream revealed that the warrior's sword had hit its mark: the *oni* disappeared, leaving its severed arm as proof of Watanabe's victory. He is said to have taken the arm and hidden it in a strongbox, refusing to show it to anyone. Stories of Watanabe do not always agree, but the arm was supposedly later stolen by a witch with the face of Hanya.

Watanabe is usually depicted with his sword drawn (some stories say it is Raiko's sword, Hige-kiri, the beard cutter), the large red *oni* just above his helmet. Raiko and his retainers, including Watanabe no Tsuna, are popular figures on kites and other Japanese art. The iconography of these warrior images is confusing, to say the least, but their powerful details and striking color show well on the many styles of Japanese kites.

Detail of a Tsugaru kite from Aomori prefecture, by unknown maker. Skinner Collection

Yoshitsune and Benkei

Examples of military heroes used as decoration on kites, Yoshitsune and Benkei are a valiant and harmonious pair whose strength and friendship are an example to all. Their meeting was not so harmonious, though; Benkei was known for ambushing knights on Kyoto's Gojo Bridge and had won the swords of 995 of them when word of his exploits reached Yoshitsune. Yoshitsune had learned the art of swordsmanship from the king of the *tengu* of his forest, and with their help he set out to vanquish Benkei.

Upon approaching the Gojo Bridge, the young Yoshitsune feigned indifference, then surprised the giant Benkei and stripped him of his weapon. With the teaching of the *tengu*, Yoshitsune avoided any blows from Benkei and mocked him with his laughter. Benkei, exhausted, tried to regain his weapon and stumbled to his hands and knees: Yoshitsune mounted the giant with a cry of triumph.

From this time forward, the two are found linked together as comrades. Their most famous exploit occurred at sea, at Dan-no-ura. Attacked by the ghosts of the Taira clan, who had been defeated in a great sea battle there, Yoshitsune cried out for revenge against the Taira dead, but Benkei quietly began to recite a number of Buddhist prayers. Peace came upon the ghosts, their wailing ceased, and they faded back into a calm sea.

Great military heroes like Yoshitsune and Benkei are often shown on the most ornate kites, in *nishike-e* brocade painting style.

Unmounted kite skin by Teizo Hashimoto. Checkley Collection, World Kite Museum

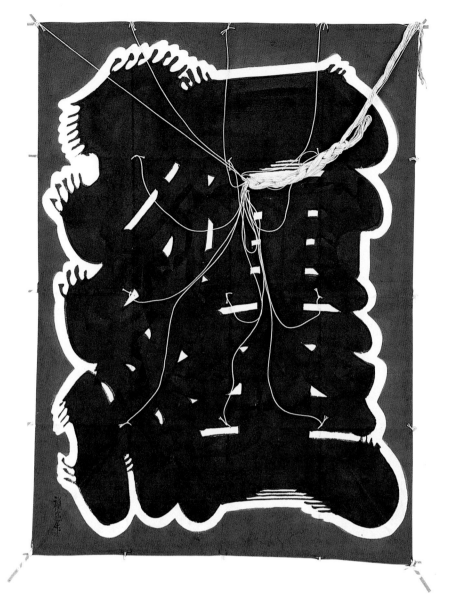

Ji-dako, or Letter Kites

In many ways, the most striking graphics found on Japanese kites are kanji characters—ideographs representing luck, beauty, strength, or even a family name. The Japanese enjoy designing kanji into their everyday surroundings: *noren* (entrance curtains), *chochin* (Japanese lanterns), *kanban* (signs), and *hanten* (*hapi* coats).

Some Words Commonly Seen on Kites

龍 *ryu:* dragon
纏 *matoi:* fireman's standard
嵐 *arashi:* storm

魁 *sakigake:* leader, forerunner,
  pioneer; into battle
蘭 *ran:* orchid

Edo kites by Teizo Hashimoto. The Tokyo Kite Museum

Tokyo maiden with a *yakko* kite. Detail from an *ukiyo-e* woodblock print
by Kuniyoshi Utagawa (1797–1861). Skinner Collection

Early Kites and Kitemakers

Masaaki Modegi

The presence of kites in Japan was first acknowledged in the records of the Shohei era (931–938), in the dictionary authored by Minamoto no Shitago, who worked under the auspices of the Imperial Department of Shinto and the Bureau of Divination. He used the Chinese name for kite, and most believe that this indicates that the kite arrived in Japan from China. These early kites were originally flown in the Kamagata area, the political and cultural center of premodern Japan, which includes the cities of Kyoto and Nara. Later, when Tokugawa Ieyasu established the shogunate in 1615, they were also flown over Edo (Tokyo), his capital.

By the year 1655, kite flying had become exceedingly popular in Japan. Enthusiasm for the practice, it seems, led to a number of brawls, which resulted in injuries. This prompted an edict prohibiting the flying of kites by children within city limits. In the following year another edict of similar content was issued.

But as time passed, the townsmen seemed to gain confidence in their kite-flying abilities, and they began to experiment with kites of various shapes, including those shaped like hawks, just as the traditional Chinese name "paper hawk" suggests. This became the most popular type of kite, as is evident in an inspection of contemporary manuscripts and picture books.

Although true Edo-ites called these kites *tombi*, etymology suggests that the word is more properly pronounced *tobi*, a term currently used to refer to men involved in dangerous occupations. During the Edo period (1615–1868) these *tobi* were firefighters who, when time allowed, served as bodyguards for the wealthiest of merchants. They were rough-and-tumble sorts; fiercely loyal, compassionate, and ready to brawl at the drop of a hat. When abused by the sword-wielding samurai, the *tobi* would strip to the waist and launch themselves, unarmed, into the fray. With their rakish chivalry, gallantry, and willingness to step in during a dispute, the *tobi* enjoyed a popularity among the common man that the samurai could not hope to attain. Because the kites represented these men, they were the first to enjoy real popularity in Edo.

Rectangular kites are most often associated with Japan. They appeared around 1716, and were most likely the brainchild of Edo-ites with a desire to somehow fly the *ukiyo-e* images then available as woodblock prints, which were becoming all the rage. The *ukiyo-e* were first refined around 1661 by Hishikawa Moronobu. The black india-ink prints *(sumizuri-e)* of the Genroku period (1688–1704) were later replaced by black prints sparingly painted in red-orange and yellow *(tan'e)*. The next stage in the development, occurring sometime after 1741, was the safflower pigment-printed picture *(benizuri-e)*, produced from two-color or three-color blocks. The final step in their evolution was the fully colored prints *(tasai-e)*, later called "brocade prints" *(nishiki-e)*.[1]

Following the end of World War II, kitemakers displayed in the major department stores kites decorated with such brocade prints. With them were found kites of the Meiji period (1868–1912) that featured a likeness of a famous kabuki actor. As a genre, these rectangular kites were called brocade-print kites *(nishikie-dako),* a label which old-time kitemaster Teizo Hashimoto prefers to the term "Edo kite," which he claims has never sat right with him.

Sometime after 1772 the footman kite *(yakko-dako)* made its appearance. This kite employed the same shape as the earlier hawk-shaped kite but was decorated to resemble *yakko,* the footmen. or servants, of the samurai, who were diligent and loyal to their lords and destined to work like beasts of burden. Footmen did everything from fetching the master's shoes and sweeping to running errands and serving as their lord's companion. The townspeople were terribly oppressed by the elite samurai, whose class privileges included the right to cut down a commoner for even so little as a perceived wrong. By flying their lowly footman kites high above the mansions of these samurai, the townsmen could at least vicariously look down on them and thumb their noses. They took great pains over the eyes of these footman images, giving them a contemptuous look and brushing them with wax so that they shone, reflecting the sunlight. The progression here is an interesting one—from the *tobi,* the townsman's chivalrous hero, to the footman, his brawl-loving elder brother. The *yakko* kites enjoy great popularity even today, being sold on New Year's Day at the Oji Inari Shrine in Tokyo as a talisman that protects one from fire. In feudal times they were often brought home as souvenirs by samurai returning to more rural areas after having served their required time in the capital. In each of these locales, the *yakko* kites have evolved in accordance with local customs and traditions.

In the Tenmei era (1781–89) the *ji-dako,* or calligraphy kite, arrived on the scene. "Edo lettering" was the name given to the unique calligraphic style that emerged from the predilections of the Edo commoners. Their idiosyncratic wielding of the brush was used on signs for plays, sumo matches, storytelling halls, and stores as well as for decorating shop curtains, banners, folding cloths, hand towels, votive cards, calendars, programs, maps, fans, and, of course, kites, where the bold letters showed up clearly. This was the time of a great famine during the corrupt government of Tanuma Okitsugu, two phenomena that led to inflation and the subsequent austerity edict of Matsudaira Sadanobu. This edict placed harsh restrictions on everything from the townspeople's clothing, combs, *ukiyo-e* prints, books, and antique works of art to everyday items and children's toys. Kites were also affected by this edict, which seems less surprising when we understand that there existed kites extravagantly decorated with gold and silver studs. Such was the time when these inexpensive calligraphy kites rose, soaring like the inflation rates.

In the Edo of ca. 1796, kites were more popular than ever. This we know from the kite specialty shops depicted in *Doji koshi* (A Child and Latticework), *Hi no de* (Sunrise), *Hanya* (Demon), and *Otafuku* (Moon-faced Woman)—small, square, childish pictures of the time, of scenes around town on New Year's Day. Kuniyoshi Utagawa, a painter whose line of succession is said to include Teizo Hashimoto, was also born around this time.[2]

The hero worship driving Kyokutei Bakin's novels *The Water Margin* and *The Tale of Three Kingdoms,* published in 1804 and 1818, proved just the right stimulus to a nation basking in peace. The subsequent boom of war and warrior tales seems to have exercised an influence on kite pictures as well.

Children's Rectangular New Year's Kites
Edo to Meiji Periods

Theme	Why Flown
Kintaro the Golden Boy Momotaro the Peach Boy	*To request of the gods strong, healthy, and successful children*
Shoki the Plague-dueler Hanya the Demon	*To ward off evil spirits*
Inari the Fox Deity Okame the Moon-faced Woman Hyottoko the Jester Daruma the Bodhidharma	*To insure safety in the home*
Shichi Fufujin, the Seven Gods of Good Fortune	*For commercial success*
Felicitous Bamboo, Pine, and Plum Crane and Tortoise of Longevity	*To celebrate auspicious occasions in the home*
The Snared Rabbit	*As an icon of wealth*

Ji-dako kite by Teizo Hashimoto featuring the kanji
character for *dragon*. The Tokyo Kite Museum

The following popular warrior pictures graced kites from the end of the Edo into the Meiji period.
These images, embodying heroism, combat, challenge, and conquest, came from novels and picture
books; kitemakers called them "armored pictures": Yoshitsune and the Eight Boats; First Man Across
the Uji River; the Struggle at Ichinotani; the Battle of Kawanajima; Watanabe no Tsuna and the Demon; Kiyomasa Quells the Tiger; Nasuno Yoichi; Yoshinaka and Lady Tomoe; the Soga Brothers; and
Benkei on Gojo Bridge.

   Popular kabuki pictures were also used on kites during this same period. Kanjincho, Shibaraku,
Kagekiyo, Ya no ne, Sukeroku, and Goro represented themes of action and excitement dramatized
in kabuki theater. Kitemakers called them "pleated pictures." While the armored pictures of warriors
were full of straight lines, pleated pictures reflected the graceful, softer lines of the kimono. It required great skill to represent strength in such pictures.

   In the skies of the "Civilization and Enlightenment Movement" of the Meiji period one-penny
kites were still being flown. Afterward, *ken-dako* kites and then *koma* (top) kites became popular.
While kites were not flown during the years of World War II, enormous, brightly colored Edo kites
rose again after the war.

Left panel of an *ukiyo-e* woodblock print triptych, possibly portraying the actor Bando Hikosaburo as the character Goro Soga. Artist unknown. Skinner Collection

Teizo Hashimoto in his workspace.

The ideograph used to represent "kite" in Japanese does not exist in the Chinese language. It came into usage sometime in the middle or late Edo period, appearing in the red-covered children's books and the yellow-covered books aimed at adult readers. It would seem that this new ideograph was created by combining two others, one meaning "phoenix" and the other "cloth."

During the years of the Civilization and Enlightenment Movement (1880s–ca. 1912), places used for kite flying were threatened, and there were signs that the practice would die out. Games played in the streets, such as kite flying, badminton, and top spinning, were considered an obstruction to traffic and were prohibited as of 1878. In their place, paper airplanes, wind-up toys, projection games, paper balloons, war games, and card-tossing gained in appeal. This was the nature of the age in which Teizo Hashimoto appeared.

Hashimoto, who died in 1993, was born in Hikifune, Mukojima, Tokyo, in 1904. When he was four years old, his family moved to an area behind the Shimotani Shrine in Ueno. Having been born into a family of kitemakers, Teizo began to help with the family business while still in elementary school. Though he learned the tricks of the trade from his father Tomekichi and his step-grandfather Fusakichi as he grew older, it was through his own concerted efforts that he secured his place as the third generation of this traditional Edo kitemaking family. Though Edo became Tokyo, there was no change in the status of kite flying: kites were flown in the older downtown district as well as in the newer, highbrow uptown Yamanote area. At this time, many kitemakers were still left.

When he was younger, Hashimoto's father worked for Hasegawa Shoten, a maker of seasonal goods whose business was located on the banks of Yanagihara in the Kanda district. There he made carp banners *(koi no bori)* for Boy's Day on May 5, fans for the hot summer months leading up to the Festival of Dead, and kites. The resident artist was Yoshitoyo Utagawa, whose son, Umemitsu, was exercising his expertise on kites.[3] He also had a friend, Sakamoto Fusakichi, a dyer by trade, who applied to paper the stenciling techniques originally used on cloth. Whereas india-ink prints had heretofore been colored by hand, this innovation allowed for the efficient mass production of multi-colored kites.

Soon after the war, in 1946, Teizo Hashimoto married Kiyo, two years his senior. She worked so hard alongside her husband that she soon developed calluses on her left hand, and yet all the while she managed to handle both the business and household affairs for this consummate craftsman. The

The Tokyo Kite Museum, interior.

entire first floor of their home, a two-story wooden structure built in the old-fashioned style, was a dedicated workshop, complete with a gap in the wall through which to sweep out the dirt. Not only was this convenient for cleaning, it also improved the ventilation in the summer and could be closed with a small door during the cold winters. This gap was also used as an entrance by the cats, which the Hashimotos, who had no children, treated lovingly as members of the family. I witnessed numerous occasions when the cats would be pawing at a ball of kite string or walking over the kites—all without a word of rebuke. On the workshop floor were scattered old paintbrushes, cans full of painting equipment, cutting boards, and Japanese paper, and overhead, above the bamboo, completed kites were visible. Realizing that among these items were some that had been used by all three generations of this family of kitemakers, one could not help but feel the weight of history.

Some of these things are on display, along with the kites, at the Tokyo Kite Museum. These kites are a piece of the common man's culture from the Edo period, a three-hundred-year stretch where the nation remained secluded from the outside world and developed a pure and uniquely Japanese culture.

Of the thirty-seven kitemakers before the war, there remains today perhaps but one. Though it is sad to think that men like Teizo Hashimoto, whose life was devoted to the Edo kite, are now gone, it is comforting to remember that both his works and photographs of them remain with us today, serving as models for kite builders all over Japan.

—translated by James Dorsey

NOTES
1. These are the gorgeous woodblock prints created through a series of color impressions. The technique was devised by the comic poet Kyosen, the painter Harunobu Suzuki, and others in 1765. *Nishiki-e* came to refer to all *ukiyo-e* prints. Outstanding artists such as Kiyonaga Torii, Utamaro Kitagawa, Toyokuni Utagawa, Hokusai Katsushika, and Hiroshige Ando cooperated with printers to expand the range of thematic materials and improve the techniques, resulting in an art genre that is now appreciated the world over.

2. Kuniyoshi Utagawa (1797–1861): *ukiyo-e* artist. An Edo-ite born in Kanda, at the age of fifteen he became a disciple of Toyokuni Utagawa I. While his popular fellow disciple Kunisada Utagawa painted pictures of beautiful women, Kuniyoshi dedicated himself to pictures of warriors. He is most famous for the series "One Hundred and Eight Heroes of the Popular *Water Margin*." From a strictly artistic perspective his scenery prints are even more renowned. He took on many students and thus left an artistic legacy that reaches into the Meiji (1868–1912) and Taisho (1912–1926) periods.

3. Yoshitoyo Utagawa I, whose real name was Kenkichi Fukuyama, also signed himself Ichiryuzai. He studied with Toyokuni Utagawa III, and later became a disciple of Kuniyoshi Utagawa. As Kunisada succeeded to the name of Toyokuni, Kuniyoshi gave Kenkichi the name Yoshitoyo as an indication that Kenkichi was his student. Yoshitoyo drew many warrior pictures as well as pictures for kites. He died in April 1866, never having married.
Yoshitoyo Utagawa II also signed himself Ichigozai. Born in 1844, his father died while Yoshitoyo was still young. He became a disciple of Yoshimoro I, and later of Yoshitoyo. In accordance with his teacher's will, he took the name Yoshitoyo in 1867. In his later years, he drew many pictures for kites.

World War II postcard. Collection of Jan and Wilma Fischer, the Netherlands

Japanese Kites, Postwar to the Present

Tsutomu Hiroi

Kites Emerge in Postwar Japan

By the war's end in 1945, Tokyo had been reduced to nothing more than a burned plain. But as early as January 1946, the first children's kite-flying contest of the postwar period was held in Hibiya Park, located in Tokyo's demolished center. Throughout the previous December, Teizo Hashimoto, proprietor of a kite shop in downtown Tokyo, had devoted many a late night to the building of kites. And a few weeks later, on New Year's Day 1946, Hashimoto was awakened by a group of excited children. The children were thrilled to now have these kites in their hands, and they enjoyed flying them over the scorched ruins of Tokyo in a traditional New Year observance.

Then, in 1947, the kite club Kyofukai was founded by fifteen or sixteen enthusiasts who styled themselves masters of the Edo rectangular kite. But this group encountered a conflict. According to member Katsuhisa Ota, there was a difference of opinion over the angle at which the kites should be flown. The "small angle" faction felt that the kites appeared more beautiful when flown at an angle close to horizontal, while the "greatest angle" faction felt that a steeper pitch showed the kites to better advantage. Unfortunately this clash of opinions led to the disbanding of the club. Later, when the Edo Kite Preservation Society was formed, Katsuhisa Ota, who flew his square kites almost horizontally, served as its first chairman.

In Japan at this time, the introduction of model airplanes in educational materials was prohibited (a restriction imposed by peace agreements with the Allies). At that time I was teaching at Tokyo Gakugei University, where most of the elementary, junior, and senior high school teachers for the Tokyo metropolitan area were trained. In my classes I instituted the design and construction of three-dimensional kites as an exercise in model design. "Light, yet strong. Able to fly in the slightest breeze and yet resilient in high winds. Kites: beautiful sculptures for the sky," was the manner in which the project was presented. The students quickly developed a succession of many new three-dimensional kites.[1]

Awa *yakko* (footman) kites, a product of the city of Tokushima on the island of Shikoku, were displayed at the Tokyo International Model-City exhibition of 1955, and attracted the attention of American buyers. The enormous orders for these kites, running into tens of thousands, represent the first step in Japan's postwar kite exports.

1960s: The National Kite Movement in Japan

In 1966 kites were included in the educational materials issued by the Japanese Ministry of Education, and an interest in kites spread throughout Japan. In 1969 Yusaku Tawara, a scholar of traditional

Launching a kite for the Hamamatsu kite battle.

Japanese arts and crafts, published *The Japanese Kite*. This hand-printed book, presented in a decorative case, was issued as a limited edition of one hundred and is now exceedingly difficult to find. (Today, more than eighty books on Japanese kites have been published.) Tawara's groundbreaking work laid the foundation for the subsequent emergence of the Japan Kite Association (J.K.A.). On November 23, 1969, fifteen kite enthusiasts in the capital held an initial organizational meeting at the Taimeiken Restaurant in Nihonbashi and formally adopted that name.

1970s–80s: Clubs and Festivals Flourish

The first Japan Kite Association competition was held in 1970 beside the Futago Bridge on the Tama River in Tokyo, with approximately 150 participants. The second competition, held that same year, drew twice that number. Today this association has over fifteen hundred members throughout Japan and issues a newsletter twice a year. Kite-flying competitions are held in every local chapter, and some chapters distribute free kites to the first two thousand arrivals.

On January 3, 1971, the mentally and physically handicapped children of Nerima Ward, Tokyo, were invited to the fields of the Japan Self-Defense Forces Ground Troops base in Nerima, where the troops and members of the Japan Kite Association coached them in their first kite-flying competition. Sponsored by the Lion's Club of Nerima, this event included the presentation to each participant of a children's rectangular kite made by kitemaster Teizo Hashimoto. The beaming smiles on the faces of these children, many of them visually impaired, as they grasped the strings of their high-flying kites, was a sight no one has forgotten. The event continues to this day.

Eighteen enthusiasts took part in a kite competition on the summit of Mt. Fuji on August 5 and 6, 1972. This event was led by Mr. and Mrs. Kashima, two experienced mountain climbers, whose marriage was a result of their mutual interest in mountaineering. The members of the expedition were Shingo Modegi, Masaaki Modegi and his wife, Katsuhisa Ota, Naotaka Fujita, Toshio Miura, Ichiro Hike and his two sons, Yoshio Isobe, Shuji Nukada, Takehiko Sato, Tsuyoshi Ogawa, Yukio Sakai and his wife, Endo (from the mountaineering club of Chuo University), and Tasuro Kashima and his wife.

Ota, the eldest member of the expedition, started out from the trail's fifth station on horseback. Around the seventh station, a chubby foreigner with saintly features noticed the equipment being carried by the group and asked, "What is all that?"

"Kites," answered a member of the expedition.

The foreigner gestured to make this next question understood: "Wow, are you planning to fly them from the summit?"

"Yes, we'll be holding the All-Japan Kite-Flying Championships there."

"That's wonderful! Give it your all, and good luck."

The group stopped at the seventh station for a nap, but the many other climbers stopping there on the way to and from the summit kept the cabin as busy as a Ginza thoroughfare all night long. Not a wink of sleep was had by anyone.

On August 6 the expedition viewed the sunrise from high on the mountain. The exquisite colors of the sky, the deep tranquillity of the world below, and the grandeur of the sun all contributed to the scene's ethereal beauty. The group set out for the summit at six o'clock. At the eighth station, they encountered a group of four old-timers, all born in the Meiji period (1868–1912), who had abandoned their quest to reach the summit. From the ninth station and beyond, they saw people who had succumbed to the high altitude and lay sprawled, sound asleep, by the side of the path, while a number of adults called out the names of energetic children who had rushed on ahead. The scene was rather chaotic.

By eleven o'clock, the kite flyers had reached the summit. Nukada was the first to arrive, and he already had his kite flying 50 meters in the air. Other members struggled with the turbulent winds. Kashima, with his newly designed kite complete with a hummer attached, had 300 meters of line out. The kite had disappeared into the clouds—a completely successful flight. Later, the group managed the descent of the mountain without incident. Their kite-flying competition was a memorable experience and a great success.

In 1973 J.K.A. members began a tradition of fellowship and education by traveling abroad with their kites. And 1974 saw the first visit to Japan by the American Kitefliers Association. On May 1, David Checkley and his son, of Seattle, and Fuo Logan and his wife, of New Zealand, arrived in Japan to participate in a J.K.A. competition. For this event, a kite was made in Yokaichi City. Its surface area was equal to eighty tatami mats (a Japanese tatami mat is approximately 95 × 190 cm), and the kite was transported to Tokyo by an enormous truck. It was successfully flown in the area of the Tama River in Tokyo.

It was arranged for the Checkleys to observe the flying of the giant kites in Hamamatsu, Showamachi, and Sagamihara. This visit became the first of an annual tradition for Mr. Checkley. Over the next fourteen years, he served as the tour leader and introduced Japanese kite flying to many Westerners.

Around this time, many outstanding kitemasters passed away, having grown old in handing down the art of traditional Japanese kitemaking. Through the passing of each and every one of these masters, we kite lovers held firmly to the belief that the heavens would watch over us. Among these masters were: Keizaburo Nakano of Hirosaki, Aomori prefecture (the Tsugaru kite); Kinjiro Hoshino of Chonam, Chiba prefecture (the *sode*, or sleeve kite); Takohachi Kato of Shizuoka City, Shizuoka prefecture (the Suruga kite); and Umeo Shiroishi of Hirado, Nagasaki prefecture (the *oni yocho*, or demon-queller kite).

Approximately one hundred locations throughout Japan are associated with the production of kites crafted in the traditional manner. While some types of kites have been lost through the ending of the line of masters that produced them, others have been revived or restored by people of the

next generation through the use of old reference materials. Among them are the *sakazuki* (sake snifter) kite of Ojiya, Niigata prefecture; the *aburi* (horsefly) and *semi* (cicada) kites of Nagoya, Aichi prefecture; the *mitsuwa* (three-ring) kite of Sukumo, Kochi prefecture; and the Baramon (Brahma) kite of Goto, Nagasaki prefecture.

On November 15, 1976, the world's first kite museum opened on the fifth floor of the Taimeiken Restaurant in Nihonbashi, Tokyo.

above: Opening of the Tokyo Kite Museum. Seated at left,
Mr. and Mrs. Teizo Hashimoto; standing, fourth from left, Shingo Modegi.
pages 64–65: Hamamatsu Kite Festival.

Shirone Kite Museum, interior atrium.

The head curator was Shingo Modegi, and the designers were Tsutomu Hiroi and Tomio Kaneko. Filling the museum was a display of kites from the collection that Modegi had acquired over many years. These men earnestly hoped that through viewing these kites, many people would come to know this fine aspect of Japan's traditional culture and enjoy themselves as well.

Around this time, a 16-millimeter film, *The Japanese Kite*, was directed and produced by Tadao Sato. It took first prize in the 1977 Cultural Film Festival.

Sixteen large hexagonal kites from Shirone, Niigata prefecture, were displayed at the organizers' request, at the Festival Dontonu in Paris, an event that marked their debut on foreign soil. On September 16, 1979, at the Seattle Cherry Blossom and Japanese Cultural Festival, ten enthusiasts from Shirone's Giant Kite Fighting Association put on a magnificent display with their giant actor kites, which measured 7.27 by 5.46 meters, or the equivalent of the area covered by twenty-four Japanese tatami mats. While in Seattle these kite flyers were guests in the home of David Checkley of the Washington Kite Association. It was an honor to execute the first demonstration of these giant Japanese kites in a foreign land.

Shirone Kite Museum, interior.

1980s: International Ties to Japanese Kites

On March 20, 1980, an attempt was made to fly a Shirone giant kite for a Guinness world record for the largest kite. The kite measured 19 by 14 meters (266 sq. m), the area of 161 tatami mats. Until that event, on May 3 and 4 of every year two giant kites, each measuring 15 by 11 meters, or 100 tatami mats, had been flown in Showa-machi, Saitama prefecture.

The 266-square-meter kite weighed 357 kilograms, despite having been built as lightly as possible. This giant kite, with a picture of the Bodhidharma's face painted on it, was raised first by a crane, then released on a signal. It flew splendidly, reaching a height of approximately 90 meters and staying aloft for twenty minutes. This size record was broken the next year in America by a cloth kite measuring 16.4 by 22.9 meters (375.56 sq. m), and again in the Netherlands by a giant kite measuring 16.3 by 32–35.38 meters (approximately 553 sq. m).

Two years later, on November 18, 1982, stuntman Ken Kazama, weighing 76 kilograms (approx. 170 lb.), was carried aloft, riding on the bridal point of a special Shirone giant kite measuring 12 by 8 meters (96 sq. m). Though his time aloft was short, he made a safe and successful flight.

In the old days, people would think, It's a beautiful day and the wind is just right. Let's go out in the fields and have some fun flying a kite! Today, though, we pick a very specific time in the future and make arrangements to fly it, perhaps even on foreign soil. The internationalization of kite flying will most likely proceed in this manner, but I hope people will not forget the way it was in the past.

On October 23, 1981, an exhibition of Japanese kites was held in London, with eight giant-kite enthusiasts from Yokaichi, Shiga prefecture, and six members of the Japan Kite Association. Just as the giant kites of Yokaichi were being sent aloft, a sudden hailstorm hit. As Hisaji Nishizawa, the leader, was attempting to fold up his giant kite, a photograph fell out of his chest pocket. Seeing that it was a picture of a Japanese woman, the crowd giggled, and Nishizawa hurriedly put it back in his pocket. The crowd could not know that it was a photograph of Nishizawa's deceased wife. Nishizawa passed away some ten years later, shortly after overseeing the opening of the Hall of Giant Kites in Yokaichi, Shiga prefecture, on May 25, 1991.

Japan's Tenth International Kite-flying Competition was held May 1, 1988, on the Miho Coast of Shizuoka prefecture. Masaaki Modegi, president of the Japan Kite Association, and Dorothea Checkley were on the stage during the opening ceremony and declared, "Welcome kite flyers both from Japan and abroad. Now, let's fly kites!" Among those present were Chris Silvia of the United States, flying from his wheelchair; Jack Van Gilder, participating with full knowledge of his incurable disease; Ro Yu San of Korea, head judge of the fighting kites; Mr. Alsa of Malaysia, with his moon kites; and Mr. and Mrs. Wayne Hosking of the United States, with their original kite creations.

The competition was blessed with clear blue skies and was a great success. Final remarks at the closing ceremony were made by David Checkley, who had decided to participate despite his illness. (He passed away on September 15 that same year.) In commemoration of this "great rainbow bridge spanning the Pacific," a plan to institute a David Checkley International Goodwill Cup was approved. The first recipient of the prize was Takeshi Nishibayashi, for his enthusiastic kite workshops in both Japan and the United States, as well as his composition of a song about kites.

Launching a *Yokaichi-odako* kite.

Kites displayed in preparation for competition at the
Hamamatsu Kite Festival.

1990s: Kite Interest Grows Stronger

On May 4 and 5, 1990, the Odako (Giant Kite) Museum opened with a flying competition in Showa-machi, Saitama prefecture. Along with the four 15-by-11-meter giant kites always on display, the museum features an extensive collection of kites from all over Japan and the world. At the time of the competition, Peter Lynn of New Zealand flew a kite shaped like a giant octopus, thereby pun-ning on the Japanese word *odako*, which means both "giant octopus" and "giant kite." For this he received the Showamachi Mayor's Award. Following the competition, at the request of honorary head curator Tsutomu Hiroi, permission was obtained from Mayor Takashi Kamiya to purchase the kite on the spot. Now prominently displayed high in the central part of the Odako Museum, it has been a source of inspiration for many Japanese children.

On January 29, 1990, Kinji Tsuda, president of the Hiroshima Kite Association, passed away at the age of seventy-six. In 1989 his group had set a world record on the sand dunes of Tottori with their chain of 24,511 kites. In addition to this world record, Tsuda was known for seizing every op-portunity to instruct children in the building of kites. He attended the Kunstdrachen (Art Kite) work-shop held at the Hiroshima Museum of Modern Art in 1988, arriving on the scene with the aid of a cane. He was so energized by the instruction that he left that day without it.

On November 18, 1990, the last great Edo kitemaster, Teizo Hashimoto, passed away at the age of eighty-seven. On November 20, 1993, with funds raised by Japan Kite Association members throughout the country, a monument to him was erected near his workplace in Taito ward, Tokyo. For the monument, a life-size phototype reproduction of his Rabbit on the Waves kite was burnt onto a piece of Arita ceramic and embedded in stone. Beneath this is engraved a thirty-one syllable poem by Hikozo Ota:

katawara no	To continue to stroke
neko o nadetsutsu	The tomcat at his side
sarigenaku	While nonchalantly
kataru wa subete	Weaving a tale—
shokunin no iki	The essence of a craftman's spirit

It was my honor to design this monument.

On January 7, 1995, the Sydney Art Kite Festival was held in Centennial Park in Sydney, Austra-lia. Kunstdrachen first exhibited these kites on June 11, 1988, in the Miyagi Prefectural Art Museum, later taking them on to the Hiroshima Museum of Modern Art. Following this, the kites went on a seven-year tour of world museums. The project, with the theme "Homo Faber—Homo Ludens"

left: Teamwork at the Hamamatsu Kite Festival.

Large Edo kite depicting Kintaro fighting a demon,
by unknown maker. Skinner Collection

(Working Man, Playing Man), was originally conceived by Dr. Paul Eubel and his assistant Ikuko Matsumoto of Osaka's German Cultural Center.

At this event, designated artists from around the world received instruction on the basic forms of traditional Japanese kites. They were chosen to make paintings for the kites on *washi*, the traditional Japanese handmade paper. These paintings were then fashioned into actual kites of varying shapes by famous kitemakers of the Japan Kite Association. The results have been published in a wonderful book.[2] The exhibition and flying demonstration of these kites left a deep impression on many people in different countries. This may very well have been the greatest role played by kites in this century. If there were a Nobel Peace Prize in the world of kites, I would surely nominate Dr. Paul Eubel and this exhibition for the award.

Though the single string which holds the kite may be fragile, I somehow feel that it firmly ties the people of the world in peace.

—translated by James Dorsey;
edited from the original manuscript
by Scott Skinner and Ali Fujino

NOTES
1. These kites were later featured in a book published by Bijutsu Publishing Company in 1972. An English translation, *Kites: Sculpting the Sky*, was issued by Pantheon Press in 1978.

2. See Paul Eubel, *Pictures for the Sky. Art Kites* (Munich: Prestel-Verlag, 1992).

left: Detail of an Edo kite by Teizo Hashimoto. The Tokyo Kite Museum

Skilled Hands: A Kite Flyer's Notebook

The kitemakers presented on the following pages represent the diversity of kite culture in Japan. Toranosuke Watanabe is one of the last traditional kitemakers in the tradition-rich region of Shirone, while Tokuko Sato follows in the kitemaking tradition of her region, the Tsugaru kite of Aomori. Mrs. Sato is one of a number of women carrying the kitemaking tradition to the next generation. Nobuhiku Yoshizumi, of Kyoto, is an active member of his traditional kite club as well as a member in the worldwide network of miniature kitemakers. Takeshi Nishibayashi uses nontraditional materials in kites that emphasize function over form. Finally, Katsutaka Murooka combines Japan's high-tech development with the Japanese kite. He is known for his kite-born aerial photography and for his sophisticated Western style adaptations of Japanese kites.

The work of these five is complemented by others active in their own ways in the modern kite movement in Japan. Whether they craft their kites from plastic garbage bags, make traditional ones of Western materials, or develop new models in traditional materials, they all contribute to the forward momentum of Japan's modern kite movement.

Flying a giant kite at the Showamachi Kite Festival.

Katsutaka Murooka

Katsutaka Murooka does not build kites in the traditional Japanese manner because he uses his kites for a very specific reason. They are lifting platforms for kite aerial photography rigs. Combining the high technology world of photography with the low-altitude perspective attained only through the use of kites, Murooka is one of a growing number of worldwide enthusiasts in the area of kite aerial photography.

Using remote-control cameras that are lifted and held stable under kites, Murooka has investigated architecture, the environment, geology, flora and fauna, the ocean, and even sporting and kiting events. He makes his own kites using Western materials: ripstop nylon and carbon-fiber spars. Many of his kites are based on traditional Japanese designs. But he also has made many Western-style kites, which are ideally suited to his camera work. Particularly beautiful and built on a grand scale is his flow-form, an inflatable soft kite, in the shape of a traditional *yakko* kite.

Murooka continues to spread information about his hobby through travel to international kite festivals and through his books, *Kite Photography* and *A Hand-Made Satellite: Kite Aerial Photography*. He is president of the Japan Kite Aerial Photography Association and continues to present workshops and demonstrations of his art.

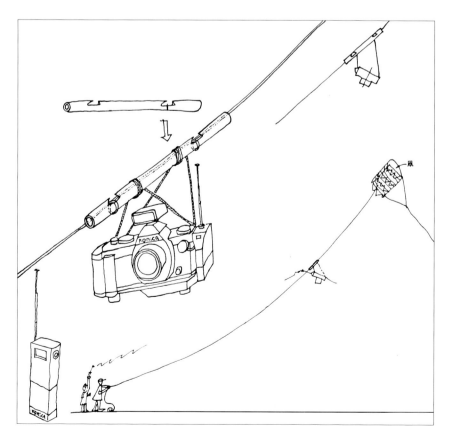

Detail of aerial kite camera harness from Murooka's sketchbook.

Takeshi Nishibayashi

Who was this wonderful man leaning out of his hotel window and singing a song I would someday come to love? His name was Nishi, shortened so that his foreign friends wouldn't have to stumble over the more formal Nishibayashi. I first met him in San Diego, in 1985. The occasion was the American Kitefliers Association annual convention, and for the third year in a row, a Japanese contingent was in attendance.

I might have overlooked Nishi's kites at first, because they were not what I had come to expect from a Japanese kitemaker: *washi* paper and bamboo, with a striking painted graphic. Instead, Nishi's kites were made with plastic sheeting, trash bags, or mylar with spars of bamboo, fiberglass, or carbon fiber and taped, glued, or folded ingeniously together. When I saw them fly, I realized the beauty of his kites—in the lightest of breezes he could make his soaring kites disappear, and with a stiffer breeze he could make his fighters dance. I soon heard stories of him flying kites behind ferryboats and making them dive in and out of the water. Takeshi Nishibayashi is anything but a traditional Japanese kitemaker, yet his kites are elegant examples of functional kites. They do exactly what they are supposed to do, with no wasted materials, no excess weight, and no excess of graphic design.

As an ambassador of kites, Nishi is without peer. He is famous for his tours of the back streets of Tokyo that invariably lead to his favorite restaurant, Beer Man's Polka. Stepping from the busy streets of Tokyo, many a foreign kite flyer has been floored by the culture shock of Beer Man's Polka, with its backdrop of German beer-hall decor, where you're liable to find a Japanese man singing Italian arias. And Nishi has a reason for bringing his friends here—he loves to sing! His favorite song, one familiar to lucky kite flyers all over the world, is his "Kite Flying" song. Characterized by an always-changing number of verses that describe various Japanese kites, Nishi's anthem is a song of international friendship. The words don't really matter; what matters is the friends that the song and its kites bring together.

Tokuko Sato

The diminutive Mrs. Sato is a dynamo when it comes to the traditional arts of Japan. She is a master in the arts of dance, song, flower arranging, and the tea ceremony. Living in the far north of Honshu Island in Aomori prefecture, Sato has also made her mark on the male-dominated worlds of martial arts and kitemaking.

In the 1960s she signed up for a single-day kite class and stayed on for four years, studying with three great craftsmen of her area, chiefly Soma Teizo. She is the living repository of Teizo's traditional knowledge, handed down over centuries (he is now deceased). Most kite flying in Aomori is done in the winter, when snow covers the ground and bone-chilling winds carry the beautiful Tsugaru kites skyward.

The rectangular Tsugaru kite is unique. It is made with a frame of cedar, rather than bamboo, and its heavy paper hummer produces noise that reverberates through the body of the kite. The *tako-e*, or kite paintings, of this form are bright, bold, and clearly distinguished from kites of other regions. The designs and decor are made to a rigid, unchanging formula; only size can vary. Mrs. Sato has made one giant Tsugaru kite. At over 8 by 10 meters, it must be stored in an apple ware-house until flown on special occasions by a large team of men—supervised, of course, by its maker.

Toranosuke Watanabe

As you walk the narrow main street of Shirone it is easy to go right past the doorway of Watanabe's kite shop. Among the nearby grocery, clothing, and hardware stores, the unassuming storefront is a gateway to traditional Japan. Since his father's death, when Watanabe was twenty-seven, he has been making kites professionally for forty-nine years; he is now seventy-six years old. He fondly remembers making kites long before his professional beginnings and proudly talks about a 2-meter *rokkaku* that he made in elementary school.

Watanabe now likes to use Korean paper for his kites because it is less expensive than Japanese paper yet is of high quality. He starts every kite painting with a *sumi-e*, a sumi-ink drawing, which is the basis for the final painting. He mixes chalk with the sumi, which produces a drawing more subtle than most and with a softer effect than many bold sumi works. As he draws the first lines of a warrior's face, he jokingly announces that the longer he draws, the more these characters begin to look like him. And he's right; when he finishes, there is a distinct resemblance that can only be noticed when the two are side by side. Watanabe's *sumi-e* are displayed throughout the workplace, because they must dry for three months before he paints color on them.

Watanabe speaks of the changes that have transpired in kitemaking during his professional career. When he was young, he traveled with his father to festivals throughout Japan. He learned how to make many styles of kites, but he now prefers the *rokkaku* of his home prefecture. He has had students but has no apprentice to follow him and carry on his family's tradition.

Nobuhiku Yoshizumi

I was introduced to Nobuhiku Yoshizumi with the simple explanation, "He makes very large kites and very small kites." Wanting to see his work, I excitedly asked to see one of his large kites and was told that he had none. The aggressive collector inside me continued to press, and I asked to see some of his miniature kites. With that, Yoshizumi produced his treasure chest of kite gems. In a box not much larger than a cigar box, he showed me a number of fine *kaku-dako* (small rectangular kites) with a variety of traditional kite images—many drawn with markers but with a wonderful translucence, unlike many painted kites. All showed that he was a fine craftsman of bamboo as well as an accomplished artist.

It was not until later that I discovered that Yoshizumi was heavily involved in making kites for the Goethe Institute's *Kunstdrachen* (Art Kites) exhibition, which features internationally known artists having their work transformed into kites by Japanese traditional kitemakers. The Kyoto Kite Association and Mr. Yoshizumi collaborated on a number of these magnificent kites, and they were the kites my friend had alluded to upon my first meeting Yoshizumi. He showed his kitemaking expertise by contributing to Edo, Tsugaru, Hachijojima, Kaku, Sagamihara, and free-form kites—all structurally different and unique to specific regions of Japan.

Yoshizumi's love is the miniature kite. He is an active member of the International Friends of Small Kites, a Dutch organization, and contributes his plans and ideas graphically, as is common in the kite world—language is not a barrier to the understanding of kites. During our first meeting, he quietly showed me a *tombi-dako* no more than six inches across. The *tombi* is a graceful, eagle-shaped kite that is difficult to make even in its full size. In miniature, its radical curves and many connections and the fine details of the bamboo frame are a testament to his skill (see illustration p. 16). It is not unusual for this kite to be presented in its own wooden case with its own reel and line.

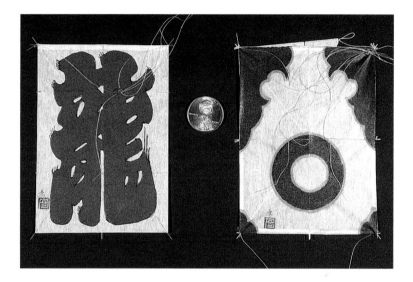

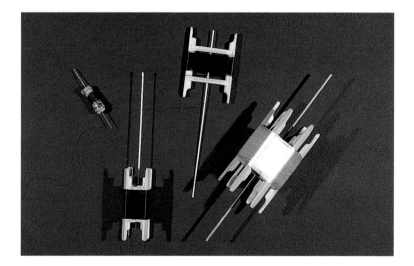

Satoshi Hashimoto

A maker of *semi-dako, abu-dako,* and similar kites, Satoshi Hashimoto feels that the most important secret of these kites is how they fly. He has confided that he would love to teach these secrets to a non-Japanese student.

Kazuo Inoue

Known for his delicate painting style, Kazuo Inoue's erotic images are complemented by the exquisite bamboo-work of their kite-canvases. His work is proof again that good things come in small packages: the kite shown is about 15 by 20 cm.

Tetsuga Kishida

Tetsuga Kishida is one of the Kunstdrachen kite builders. He has built a fully collapsible *Edo-dako* of traditional materials, thereby combining today's wish for portability with yesterday's traditions of fine detail and craftsmanship.

Shoji Kobayashi

Another of the Sanjo *rokkaku* kitemakers of the Shirone region, Shoji Kobayashi's *rokkaku* are noticeably different in style from those of Toranosuke Watanabe. *Rokkaku* are loved by Westerners hunting for original Japanese kites —they collapse and roll up, making them easy to transport home.

Seiko Nakamura

A kite ambassador for his city and a fine builder of the *Nagasaki-hata,* Seiko Nakamura has designed this *hata*-style bee kite. It is reminiscent in design of the red-white-and-blue *hata,* but its bold graphics are unique and instantly recognizable.

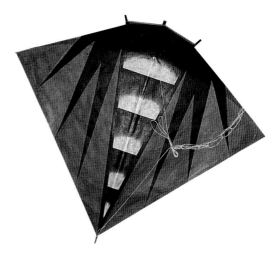

Akihiro Ogawa

A professional kitemaster of the traditional *Nagasaki-hata,* Akihiro Ogawa is recognized as the finest maker of the striking *hata* kite. Flying characteristics must be the first priority for the kitemaker, but his bold geometric designs are easily distinguishable during the heat of kite battle.

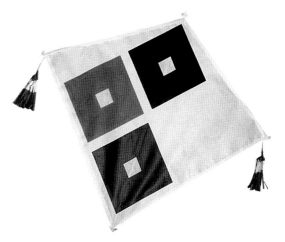

Eiji Ohashi

For years Eiji Ohashi has been famous for his trains of kites, but he should be recognized for his innovative approach to kitemaking as well. He uses traditional or modern materials, and his books on Japanese kites, with their clear plans and illustrative details, are useful to any enthusiast.

Mitsuaki Ohtsuka

When flying on the grounds of the Shirone Kite Museum, Mitsuaki Ohtsuka, of the Niigata Bird Kite Club, flies his three-dimensional condor. The active Niigata club is always present at festivals in the Shirone area.

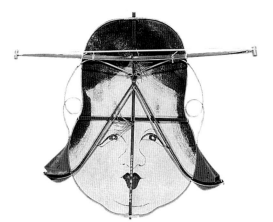

Masaaki Sato

It's always a thrill to see Masaaki Sato's box of kites. He exposes little of what's inside, making every kite a separate surprise when pulled out to fly. He has helped to reveal many of the lost secrets of Nagoya's insect kites, but I fell in love with Okame.

Teruo Suga

Teruo Suga is a charming kitemaker, who specializes in miniature kites. On our last meeting, I learned that the Edo-period name for miniature kites was *suga*, thus, Mr. Suga knowingly or by circumstance carries on the tradition of making *suga-dako*—in this case, small kites by Suga.

Morihiro Takeda

Morihiro Takeda, an avid collector of modern and traditional kites, is a welcome participant at kite auctions worldwide. Expanding his interests, he has commissioned Japanese-style kites in modern materials—at present, one for each member of his family. Traditional in style, but made of cotton fabrics that Takeda uses in his clothing business, the kites are models of modern ideas applied to traditional Japanese kites.

Kazuo Tamura

If you're lucky enough to find the *National Geographic* footage on the kite battles on Shirone, you will soon come to know Kazuo Tamura. On the kite battlefield, his shrill voice is that of a respected leader, but away from the field he was the driving force behind the creation of the Shirone Kite Museum. Through his many travels and demonstrations of giant Shirone kites, Mr. Tamura has made friends worldwide.

Kazue Tanaka

Kazue Tanaka's small *tombi*-style birds incorporate the intricate structure critical to the kite's design while featuring delicate and realistic painting that can easily fool the casual observer into momentarily thinking the image is a real bird.

Mr. Taniguchi

China is an unlikely place to find a Japanese kitemaker, yet that is where I met Mr. Taniguchi. The Baramon kite shown is traditionally from Goto Island and hearkens back to Chinese art traditions.

Toki

A dynamic young kitemaker, Toki specializes in traditional kites of the Edo region. While in New Zealand, I was fascinated to watch him as he conducted a workshop—using a minimum of English—on the *koma* (spinning top) kite. The personable Toki has displayed his skills at Disney's Epcot Center and has treated American kite flyers with his kites at their national convention.

Terauki Tsutsumi

Resident kitemaker of the Tokyo Kite Museum, Terauki Tsutsumi makes a beautiful *tombi-dako*. The intricate bamboo-work is exceptional, and the kite is magical in flight as it draws real eagles to share thermals.

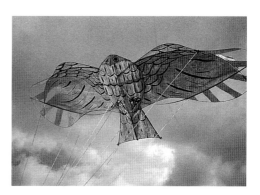

Japanese Kite Festivals

Fujisaki, Aomori prefecture
Dates: Second Sunday in February, last Sunday
   in April
Contact: Aomori Branch, Japan Kite Association*
Description: In February the Fujisaki Festival features
   the beautiful, traditional Tsugaru kite. In April it
   shares the flying field with contemporary kite
   inventions and kites made by Japan's finest kitemakers. Members of the Japan Kite Association
   mingle with prominent kite personalities and invited guests from abroad. Some of these renowned
   kitemakers employ the most up-to-date concepts
   and materials available. Their kites bear images of
   everything from traditional motifs to innovative
   concepts in art.—T.S.

Hamamatsu, Shizuoka prefecture
Date: Golden Week, early May
Contact: Hamamatsu Festival Hall**
Description: The Hamamatsu Kite Festival, full of
   color, pageantry, and passion, is Japan's largest.
   It attracts an annual audience estimated at two
   million. as kite teams battle for dominance of the
   sky over city neighborhoods. In recent times over
   150 neighborhood teams have crowded into Hamamatsu's Wajiyama Park flying field. The kites are
   spectacular, and the flying events can only be
   described as wild, mind-numbing pandemonium.
   Hamamatsu traces its kite-flying tradition back to
   its founding in 1670; town historians date the first
   full-fledged kite battles there to around 1887.
       Hamamatsu is two-and-a-half hours south of
   Tokyo on the Shinkansen, the bullet train, out of
   Tokyo Station.—T.S.

Hoshubana, Saitama prefecture
Date: Golden Week, early May
Contact: Mr. Chunosuke Teshima, Saitamakenminami
   Branch, Japan Kite Association*
Description: The Hoshubana *odako* is among Japan's
   largest kites, and its launching is a highlight of this
   festival. It measures 11 by 15 meters and weighs
   800 kilograms. Its bamboo frame is covered by
   fifteen hundred sheets of strong Japanese rice
   paper. These giant kites have been flown without
   fail for the last 260 years.

Until a Dutch version of the West's modern
Jalbert parafoil kite claimed the record in the late
1980s, the *odako* of Hoshubana and *Yokaichi* had
long been acknowledged as the largest kites in
the world.—T.S.

Ikazaki, Ehime prefecture
Date: October
Contact: Ikazaki Kite Museum**
Description: Features the fighting *ho-dako*, or
   sail kites.

Junction, Texas, USA, Kite Retreat
Date: Memorial Day weekend, end of May
Contact: Betty Street, Texas Tech University, Lubbock,
   Texas, USA
Description: This annual gathering of kite enthusiasts
   brings together noted kite artisans from around the
   world. Japanese kitemakers are usually featured
   presenters and guests.

Kumamoto, Kumamoto prefecture
Date: fall
Contact: Japan Kite Association*
Description: Features distinctive Baramon-style kites
   and kites of southern Japan.

Nagasaki, Nagasaki prefecture
Date: Dates vary from March through May
Contact: Mr. Seiko Nakamura, 958-45-7239
Description: Nagasaki is famous for its *hata* fighting
   kite, which is similar to the fighting kite of India.
   Small, red-white-and-blue *hata* with ground-glass-
   coated flying lines mix it up in friendly fighting
   matches for prizes in organized competitions and
   informally for pure fun.—T.S.

Naruto, Tokushima prefecture
Date: June–July
Contact: Mr. Umeo Fujinaka
Description: A spectacular opportunity to see the
   giant, round *wan wan* kites.

Sagamihara, Kanagawa prefecture
Date: Golden Week, early May
Description: Two sizes of kite are customarily flown at
   Sagamihara. The larger measures 14.4 meters on a
   side and tips the scale at 950 kilograms. Though

known as the Sagamihara *odako*, this kite is actually made in Isobe. Sagamihara shares an *odako*-flying festival with the neighboring community of Zama.—T.S.

Shirone, Niigata prefecture

Date: June 2

Contact: Kazuo Tamura, Shirone Kite Museum**

Description: Large kites from Shirone and Ajikata fight over the Nakanokuchi River; the event culminates in a team tug-of-war. Shirone also flies the six-sided *Sanjo rokkaku-dako* along with the neighboring community of Sanjo. Both the giant kites and the *rokkaku* are flown as fighting kites.—T.S.

Showamachi, Saitama prefecture

Date: Golden Week, early May

Contact: Showamachi Kite Museum**

Description: The traditional Showamachi giant kite is flown during this festival. It is an opportunity to see one of Japan's giant kites and the enthusiastic crowds that attend to celebrate its flight. Showamachi is not far from Tokyo.

Uchinada, Ishikawa prefecture

Date: Golden Week, early May

Contact: Mr. Masaaki Modegi, The Tokyo Kite Museum**

Description: This international festival draws kite flyers from every region of Japan, as well as international guests, flying the finest of contemporary kites. This is the best opportunity to see many different Japanese kites at one location.

Washington State International Kite Festival, Long Beach, Washington, USA

Date: third full week of August

Contact: Kay Buesing, World Kite Museum**

Description: This West Coast US festival is the largest in North America and features internationally known kitemakers as well as regional flyers and makers. Japanese kite flyers frequently attend as guests to fly their traditional kites. Japanese kites can always be seen at the World Kite Museum, also located in Long Beach.

Yokaichi, Shiga prefecture

Date: Last Sunday in May

Contact: Yokaichi World Kite Museum**

Description: The *Yokaichi-odako* is one of the more exquisitely formed and designed of Japan's giants. Thin pieces of cut bamboo are shaped and fitted around traditional design elements (for example, birds or fish; a new design is created each year) and incorporate well-designed calligraphy.

The *odako* team spreads out along the length of the kite's thick rope flying line and then races across a dry riverbed strewn with big boulders to launch the kite, which rises slowly and majestically until it is caught by the wind.

In 1995 the Yokaichi kite was honored by the Japanese government and designated as an Intangible National Property.—T.S.

Zama, Kanagawa prefecture

Date: Golden Week, early May

Description: Giant kites are flown along the Sagami River. City floats add to the festivities.

*See Appendix C: Japan Kite Association Branches.
**See Appendix B: Kite Museums with Japanese Kite Collections.

Kite Museums with Japanese Kite Collections

Hamamatsu Festival Hall

Address: 1313 Nakatajimacho, Hamamatsu City, Shizuoka 340, Hamamatsu, Japan

Phone: 05434-41-6211

The festival hall contains a small *dashi*, one of the shrines used in the city parades during Golden Week. It also contains many kites and good information about the kite battle.

Ikazaki Kite Museum

Address: 1437 Furutako Ooaza Ikazakicho, Kitagun, Ehime 795-03, Ikazaki, Japan

Phone: 0893-44-5200

Fax: 0893-44-5202

This is a new museum, with kites from Japan and foreign countries and wonderful historical photos of the Ikazaki Kite Festival. Nearby the museum, a traditional papermaker has a workshop that is well worth visiting.

Shirone Odako to Rekishinoyakata

Address: 1770-1 Suwaki Kamishimo Ooaza, Shirone City, Niigata 950-12, Shirone, Japan

Phone: 025-372-0315

Fax: 025-378-0316

Another new museum, this large, beautiful building holds full-size Shirone kites, an extensive collection of Japanese kites (well labeled), and many unique foreign examples. The building even has a wind tunnel for kite testing.

Showamachi Odako Kaikan (Kite Museum)

Address: 637 Nishihoshubana Oaza Showamachi Kitakatsushikagun, Saitama 344-01, Showamachi, Japan

Phone: 048-748-1555

Fax: 048-748-1330

Four full-size Showamachi *odako* are the highlight of this museum. The museum also contains some foreign examples.

The Tokyo Kite Museum

Address: 1-12-10, Nihonbashi, Chuo-ku, Tokyo, Japan T 103

Phone: 33-275-2704

Fax: 33-273-0575

This might be a kite enthusiast's first destination in Japan. The collection includes miniatures capable of flight and every other size of kite including the giant *odako*, as well as the full range of kite forms found across Japan. The museum also houses an extensive collection of historical documents and *ukiyo-e* kite pictures.

Founded by Shingo Modegi as a privately funded museum open to the public, it is now directed by his son Masaaki Modegi, a tireless champion, patron, and participant in kite activities throughout the world.

The world's first kite museum, it remains a model and resource for the amazing community-sponsored public kite museums that have recently blossomed in Japan.—T.S.

Yokaichi World Kite Museum

Address: 3-5 Higashihoncho, Yokaichi City, Shiga 527, Yokaichi, Japan

Phone and Fax: 0748-23-0081

Included in the Japanese kite collection here are examples of the unique Yokaichi *odako*.

World Kite Museum and Hall of Fame

Address: 104 North Pacific Avenue, Long Beach, Washington, USA 98631

Phone: 360-642-4020

Fax: 360-642-2318

The World Kite Museum houses the finest collection of Japanese kites outside Japan—the David Checkley collection. Long Beach is also the site of the Washington State International Kite Festival (during the third full week of August) and often has Japanese kite-flying guests.

Japan Kite Association Branches

If you are planning to travel to Japan and are interested in learning more about Japanese kites, you can contact any of the Japan Kite Association branches to receive information about the kites of that particular area.

Adachi Branch
Attn.: Mr. Morihiro Takeda
Address: 2-37, Senju Adachiku, Tokyo
Phone: 03-3881-5194

Akitaken Kodamakai Branch
Attn.: Mr. Minoru Ito
Address: 212-1, Nibanseki idetocho, Honjo City, Akita
Phone: 0184-22-2732

Aomori Branch
Attn.: Mr. Hiroshi Takehana
Address: 34-20, Aza Izumikawa Namiyakata Ooaza, Aomori City, Aomori
Phone: 0177-77-8098

Aomoriken Chukounankoku Branch
Attn.: Mr. Keizo Nakano
Address: 197 Watokucho Hirosaki City, Aomori
Phone: 0172-32-7033

Bibai Branch
Attn.: Mr. Masahiro Takeichi
Address: c/o Marukatsu Takeichi Co., Bibai City, Hokkaido, 5-1-3, Higashiyonjo Kita
Phone: 01266-2-6211

Chiba Branch
Attn.: Mr. Tomio Tsunezumi
Address: 1167 Ushiku, Ichihara City, Chiba
Phone: 0436-92-0268

Hakodate Branch
Attn.: Mr. Shusei Akiyama
Address: 27-1, Fukaboricho, Hakodate City, 042 Hokkaido
Phone: 0138-51-1992

Hiroshima Branch
Attn.: Mr. Kazuto Murai
Address: 1-13-15 Yamadashinmachi, Nishiku, Hiroshima City, Hiroshima
Phone: 082-273-0382

Honjo Branch
Attn.: Mr. Kiyonori Sato
Address: 209-1, Nibanseki, Idetocho, Honjo City, Tokyo prefecture
Phone: 01842-2-3879

Hyogo Branch
Attn.: Mr. Masayuki Yamaguchi
Address: 4-44-10, Andojicho, Itami City, Hyogo
Phone: 0727-81-3883

Ibaraki Branch
Attn.: Mr. Akira Ishiyama
Address: 1612 Ooaza Hokota Hokotacho, Kashimagun, Ibaraki
Phone: 0291-3-4027

Itabashi Branch
Attn.: Mr. Shigeo Okita
Address: 5-22-2, Akatsuka Itabashi, Tokyo
Phone: 03-3930-0250

Kagawa Branch
Attn.: Mr. Masayuki Yamaji
Address: 1052-2, Kinzojicho, Zentsuji City, Kagawa
Phone: 0877-28-7907

Kagoshima Branch
Attn.: Mr. Sadao Harada
Address: 3-28-19, Take, Kagoshima City, Kagoshima
Phone: 0992-51-3655

Kitanotako Branch
Attn.: Mr. Nobuo Ichinohe
Address: 10-15-2, Rokujo Nishino Nishiku, Sapporo
City, Hokkaido
Phone: 011-662-5002

Koda Branch
Attn.: Mr. Koichi Hiraiwa
Address: 12-6, Aza Kusunoki Sakazaki Kodacho,
Nukatagun, Aichi
Phone: 0424-67-0213

Marugame Branch
Attn.: Mr. Fumiaki Yukinari
Address: 1148-1 Gunyacho, Marugame City,
Marugame
Phone: 0877-28-7907

Mie Branch
Attn.: Mr. Kanaya Moriya
Address: 3648-2, Sainomiya Meiwacho
Takigun, Mie
Phone: 05965-2-0628

Naruto Oodako Hozonkai Branch
Attn.: Mr. Umeo Fujinaka
Address: 10-3, Rokunokoshi Yakura Otsucho,
Naruto City, Tokushima
Phone: 0868-86-1567

Niigata Branch
Attn.: Mr. Katsumi Arai
Address: 2-54, Hamauracho, Niigata City, Niigata
Phone: 0252-67-0213

Osaka Branch
Attn.: Mr. Masao Hashimoto
Address: 1-99-3, Morofuku, Daito City, Osaka
Phone: 0720-71-5485

Saitamakenminami Branch
Attn.: Mr. Chunosuke Teshima
Address: 3-14-14 Tsurusenishi, Fujimi City, Saitama
Phone: 0492-51-8340

Samani Branch
Attn.: Mr. Katsunori Saito
Address: Samanicho Yakubanai 1-21, Odori
Samanicho, Hokkaido
Phone: 01463-6-2662

Shimotsuke Branch
Attn.: Mr. Kiyoshi Kobayashi
Address: 2739 Ishicho, Utsunomiya City, Tochigi
Phone: 0286-61-32016

Tokai Branch
Attn.: Mr. Matsuo Aizawa
Address: 178 Hirade Futagoaza Ooaza Shikatsucho
Nishi Kasugaigun, Aichi
Phone: 0568-21-2623

Tokushima Branch
Attn.: Mr. Hiroichi Kudo
Address: 1-5-1 Fukushima, Tokushima City, Tokushima
Phone: 0886-53-6450

Tokushima Takonokai Rengokai Branch
Attn.: Mr. Tetsu Sasayama
Address: c/o Sogo Keikaku Kiko, Shinyoshino Bld.
2-46, Mishimacho Hokuzyo, Tokushima City,
Tokushima
Phone: 0886-55-5570

Toyama Branch
Attn.: Mr. Mitsuo Mikawa
Address: 1287 Futakuchi Daimoncho Imizugun,
Toyama
Phone: 0766-52-1776

Tsugaru Branch
Attn.: Mr. Yoshizo Sakuraba
Address: 30-2 Ten m Ooaza, Aomori City, Aomori
Phone: 0177-77-8098

Tsugaru Kite Branch
Attn.: Mr. Jinya Sato
Address: 17 Honcho Fujisakicho Minami, Tsugarugun
038-38 Aomori prefecture
Phone: 0172-75-4020

Wakayama Branch
Attn.: Mr. Katsuhiko Kaburagi
Address: 150 Enokihara, Wakayama City, Wakayama
Phone: 0734-55-2466

Yokohama Branch
Attn.: Mr. Tomio Kaneko
Address: 5-11 Nishimachi Isogoku, Yokohama City,
Kanagawa
Phone: 045-761-5555

Glossary

abu-dako — Horsefly kite traditionally made in Nagoya

Baramon (Brahma) — Figure kite typical of the island of Goto

bekkako — A funny face, usually with its tongue sticking out

Boy's Day — May 5 (now Children's Day), a time for many traditional kite festivals

buka — Refers to the sound certain kites make when they rise; also, a fighting kite from Mori, a town in Shizuoka prefecture

Daruma — Japanese name for the Bodhidharma

Edo-dako — Rectangular kite from the Tokyo area

fengzheng — Wind harp; Chinese generic term for kite

fugu — Blowfish

Fujin — God of wind

hachi-dako — Bee kites traditionally made in Nagoya

hachimaki — Folded or rolled headband often seen on workmen and kite flyers

hakkaku — Octagonal or eight-pointed star

Hamamatsu — Traditional kite battle town in Shizuoka prefecture

Hanya — A female demon said to frighten away evil spirits

hapi coat — Short coat often worn when flying kites, adorned with club, neighborhood, or personal designs

hata — Flag; popular generic term for kite (more correctly, the Nagasaki fighter kite)

hiba — Japanese cypress; used in Aomori's Tsugaru kites

ho-dako — Sail kite of Ikazaki

ika-dako — Squid kite

Ikazaki — Southern Japanese city with unique fighting kite: the name of the kite is "Sail," and it resembles a rectangular sail and mast

iwai-dako — Celebration kite

jomon or *mon* — Family crest

ji-dako — Kanji kite; a kite decorated by a Japanese ideograph

kaku-daku — Generic term for rectangular kite

kazusa Tojin — Fertility kite from Chiba prefecture

kenka kite — A style of fighter kite flown in the town of Taharu, Aichi prefecture

kerori — Five-sided kite that looks like a bow tie

Kintaro — Golden Boy; often seen riding a carp

ko-dako — Children's kite

koi no bori — Carp windsock, associated with Children's Day

koma-dako — Spinning-top kites

Machijirushi — "District kite," like those from neighborhoods in Hamamatsu

makiika — Literally, rolled squid; it sometimes refers to the ability of a Sanjo *rokkaku* to be rolled for transport

nishiki-e — Brocade picture; with *tako*, a color-print kite

odako — A large kite, like those of Showamachi

Okame — Goddess of mirth and laughter

oniyozu — Demon kite

rokkaku — Hexagonal; normally used as a name for the six-sided kites of Shirone, also called *Sanjo-rokkaku*

Sagara — Fighting-kite festival town with Sagara kite or *kenka* kite

Shirone — Town known for battles between giant kites

semi-dako — Cicada kites; traditionally made in Nagoya

sode — Literally, sleeve; the name for the kimono-shaped kite of Chiba prefecture

sumi-e — Black-ink outline that defines the kite picture; then painted with colors made from powdered, water-soluble dyes

Suruga — Kite with two square corners at the top, widening to three points at the bottom; from Shizuoka prefecture

take — Bamboo

tako — Octopus; common generic term for kite

tako kichi — Kite-crazy; a disease afflicting the vast majority of kite flyers

tombi or *tobi* — Hawk, or hawk kite, traditionally made in Tokyo

tosa — Collapsible diamond-shaped kite from Kochi prefecture

Tsugaru — Rectangular kite from northern Japan, made with cypress, instead of bamboo

unari — Hummers; devices that travel up and down the flying line of an airborne kite, making weird noises as they go

wan wan — Round kite from Tokushima prefecture

washi — Handmade paper made from fibers of the mulberry plant

yakko — A samurai's retainer; the "footman" kite, made in human shape

Bibliography

Baten, Lea. *Playthings and Pastimes in Japanese Prints*. New York: Weatherhill, 1995.

Davis, F. Hadland. *Myths and Legends of Japan*. London: Harrap and Co., 1912.

Eubel, Paul. *Pictures for the Sky. Art Kites*. Munich: Prestel-Verlag, 1992.

Govig, Valerie. "To Kyushu with Kites," *Kite Lines* (Spring 1988): 68–79.

Hiroi, Tsutomu. *Tako: sora no zokei* (Kites: Sculpting the Sky). Tokyo: Bijutsu Shuppan-sha, 1972. English edition—New York: Random House, 1978.

Kung, David. *Japanese Kites, A Vanishing Art*. Tokyo: 1962 (self-published).

Legend in Japanese Art: A Description of Historical Episodes, Legendary Characters, Folk-lore Myths, Religious Symbolism. London and New York: John Lane Company, 1908.

Modegi, Masaaki, ed. *Edo-dako dai zenshu* (Great Collection of Edo Kites). Tokyo: Sankaido, 1988.

————. *Edo-dako: Hashimoto Teizo no sekai* (Edo Kites: The World of Hashimoto Teizo). Tokyo: Seibundo, Shinkosha, 1986.

Murooka, Katsutaka. *Kite Photography*. Tokyo: Shashin Kogyo Publishers, 1989.

Peters, George. "Hamamatsu: Festival of Festivals," *Kite Lines* (Winter 1992–93): 26–30.

Poehler, Carl, Jr. "The Miracle of Sagamihara," *Kite Lines* (Winter 1979–80): 42–43.

Streeter, Tal. *The Art of the Japanese Kite*. New York and Tokyo: 1974 (5th printing, 1985).

Symmes, Edwin C., Jr. *Netsuke, Japanese Life and Legend in Miniature*. Rutland, Vermont, and Tokyo: Charles E. Tuttle, 1991.

Tamura, Kazuo (trans. Dan Kurahashi). "The Shirone Giant Kite Battle," *Kite Lines* (Spring 1984): 20–22.

Tawara, Yusaku. *The Japanese Kite*. Tokyo: Kikkasha, 1970.

About the Authors

Tal Streeter

A sculptor and teacher, Tal Streeter studied with Robert Motherwell and apprenticed with the sculptor Seymour Lipton in New York. During the early 1970s he traveled through Japan, India, and Korea, where he encountered the windborne art of the kite. When Streeter returned to the United States in 1973, he founded the IID/Media Sculpture section of the Visual Arts Department at the State University of New York, Purchase, where he still teaches.

Streeter produces sculpture on a grand scale—works that in many cases use the sky as their canvas. He is fascinated by art that interacts with its environment, and his kite projects have included the *Flying Red Line*—a massive parafoil lifting a tail that stretched to the horizon—and a series of Japanese-style kites, all with the Red Line theme. Over the last twenty years, his sculptures, installations, and events have been mounted throughout the United States and abroad. Streeter continues to be involved in kites through his world travels and is the author of *The Art of the Japanese Kite* (1974) and *Kites: A Journey Through India* (1996).

Scott Skinner

A 1975 graduate of the U.S. Air Force Academy, Scott Skinner became interested in kites as a creative release from flying. Upon his resignation from the Air Force, he took over management of family investments and became more active in kiting events. Travels to China in 1988 and Japan in 1989 sparked his appreciation for traditional Asian kites, which he has collected extensively. In addition, he is interested in all things depicting kites, including Japanese *ukiyo-e* prints, European bookplates, ceramics, glassware, sculpture, and paintings. He is an award-winning kitemaker, combining the flat, geometric shapes of Japanese kites with traditional American patchwork patterns, and translating common Japanese artistic images into abstract geometric motifs.

In 1994 Skinner founded the Drachen Foundation, a nonprofit educational corporation dedicated to the increase and diffusion of kite knowledge by teaching historical, cultural, scientific, and artistic aspects of kiting. The Foundation supports educational publications, exhibits, workshops, and artist-in-residence programs with kites as their focus.

Masaaki Modegi

Head of the Japan Kite Association and director of the Tokyo Kite Museum, Masaaki Modegi is a tireless champion, patron, and participant in kite activities throughout the world and is Japan's unofficial ambassador of kites. He travels extensively and has added to the Tokyo Kite Museum's collection by searching out premium examples of contemporary kites from around the world. He takes Japanese kitemakers with him to international kite festivals, meetings, and workshops, including the American Kitefliers Association convention, which he has attended since 1983.

Modegi is an avid photographer, and he promotes local and international events by publishing articles and photos in the *JKA Newsletter*. His All-Japan Kite Festival, normally held in Uchinada, is one of the few places where international guests can see Japanese kites from every corner of the country. Professionally, Modegi has followed in the footsteps of his father, Shingo Modegi, as head chef at the Taimeiken Restaurant in Tokyo's Ginza district. He has published cooking articles, cookbooks, and guides to fine eating in Tokyo.

Tsutomu Hiroi

Tsutomu Hiroi came to kites through a life-long interest in flying objects—paper airplanes, model airplanes, hot air balloons, and kites. As an artist and sculptor, he saw the potential for kites as sculptural art and used them as teaching tools for his design students. His book, *Kites: Sculpting the Sky* (English edition, 1978), was a welcome addition to kite flyers' libraries worldwide. Hiroi was a founding member of the Japan Kite Association and was instrumental in designing the Tokyo Kite Museum, which is located in Shingo Modegi's Taimeiken Restaurant.

To anyone interested in box kites, Professor Hiroi's ideas of twenty years ago still provide inspiration—they show the beauty and flexibility of a cellular approach to construction. Hiroi continues to be active in kite flying. He frequently accompanies foreign guests to Japanese kite festivals, where he flies his own creations, which he also flies purely for his own enjoyment.